Hero/
Villain

Also by Mark Eglinton

No Domain: The John McAfee Tapes

Hero/ Villain

Satoshi : The Man Who Built Bitcoin

Mark Eglinton

PERMUTED
PRESS

A PERMUTED PRESS BOOK
ISBN: 979-8-88845-427-5
ISBN (eBook): 979-8-88845-428-2

Hero/Villain:
Satoshi: The Man Who Built Bitcoin

Cover design by Heath Kane

This is a work of nonfiction. All people, locations, events, and situations are portrayed to the best of the author's memory.

PERMUTED
PRESS
Permuted Press, LLC
New York • Nashville
permutedpress.com

Published in the United States of America
1 2 3 4 5 6 7 8 9 10

TABLE OF CONTENTS

PROLOGUE

When an individual or group of individuals operating under the pseudonym Satoshi Nakamoto published a white paper entitled *Bitcoin: A Peer-to-Peer Electronic Cash System* on October 31st, 2008, a shockwave reverberated through the close-knit cryptography community. This white paper, which numbered just nine pages including references, described the principles behind a revolutionary system of digital cash whereby "a purely peer-to-peer version of electronic cash would allow online payments to be sent directly from one party to another without going through a financial institution" could exist. Nakamoto further stated that the background work on the computer code underpinning Bitcoin had begun in 2007.

Prior to the publication of the white paper on a niche cryptography mailing list located at metzowd.com, an internet domain entitled bitcoin.org was registered. Everything had been carefully orchestrated; Bitcoin was ready to roll out.

As exciting as Satoshi's white paper was in the sense that the ideas it presented seemed uniquely watertight, it was received with a degree of side-eyed suspicion. The cryptographic community—a cynical bunch at the best of times—was entirely accustomed to pretenders appearing on the scene with promising schemes that later failed. Many such examples had come and gone over the years. What was different was that, although Satoshi's idea was not the first attempt at a digital cash system (well-known ventures like DigiCash and E-Gold had tried and failed previously) all the concepts described by the white paper regarding triple-entry accounting and solutions to historical roadblocks like "double-spending" seemed definitive in a way that previous iterations hadn't. And that wasn't all. Beyond the specifics was something bigger, something more cinematic in scope.

Satoshi's white paper—for the niche few aware of it at that time—offered a clear-eyed view of a world beyond financial middlemen that didn't so much seek to create an anarchic movement designed to rail against the central banks, but instead would permit a new means of transacting quickly, inexpensively, and across borders. These intentions were both positive and potentially revolutionary. Bitcoin, as it was originally characterized by Satoshi's vision, was as much about a better future for mankind as the invention of the wheel had been in circa 4200BC.

But nothing nowadays is ever that simple.

Sadly, Satoshi Nakamoto's mere existence just wasn't enough for the hordes of disciples. In fact, ever since the Satoshi pseudonym broke cover in 2008, debate has raged constantly in mainstream media and in niche Bitcoin fixated groups on sites like Reddit about not just who or what is behind the persona, but also about what the contents of the document actually mean. Other than communicating in what expert analysts concluded was uncomplicated "British-style" English, using curse words like "bloody" and expressions such as "flat" instead of apartment, few other linguistic clues were left that could provide definitive identification.

Predictably, multiple theories have come and gone in the years since as to who might be behind the moniker and many people have taken it upon themselves to try to find out. But every time a major publication sent someone out to find the internet's own Big-foot, some beleaguered reporter returned with news of a sighting of something else. *Forbes*, *Newsweek*, *The New York Times*, *Vice*, and *The New Yorker* all threw their hats into the Satoshi ring over the years. All came up with something, just not the real Satoshi Nakamoto.

A range of individuals have inevitably been pushed forward as potential candidates—a dozen or so that could be classed as viable contenders. Dorian Nakamoto, Nick Szabo, Hal Finney, and Adam Back were just a few such suspects from within the computer science world. Elon Musk, convicted criminal Paul Le Roux, Silk Road alleged founder Ross Ulbricht, and even the US Government itself have been offered up as suspects. One by one, however, they would all be debunked and dismissed when the key facts just didn't stack up when exposed to a little basic online research. For journalists, attempting to unmask Satoshi Nakamoto became a frustrating fool's errand at best, and a perilous credibility-jeopardizing endeavor at worst.

Meanwhile, the *real* Nakamoto remained elusive, having stepped away from all public discussions about Bitcoin in 2011, in the process leaving their invention at the mercy of those who sought to manipulate it to suit their own agendas. But, even in absentia, Satoshi Nakamoto continued to live rent free in the Bitcoin community's collective heads. Consequently, instead of focusing only on what Bitcoin could actually do, "Bitcoiners," tech experts, and even high-brow academics also pored over the intricate details of both Satoshi's computer code and the many written communications between 2008 and 2011, all in an attempt to both identify him or her and to find fallibilities that might discredit the concept in some great "A-ha!" moment. Along the way, individuals have been doxxed, fled countries, and died.

In parallel, the concept of cryptocurrency—much more as a hoardable investment proposition like gold than the peer-to-peer payment system Bitcoin was intended to be—became an integral part of the vernacular and daily life. IPOs (coins, basically) of all kinds appeared from out of the woodwork; cryptocurrency exchanges materialized as a means to swap these coins or convert them to cash. Some of these exchanges have since crashed, leaving investors without their cryptocurrency and nothing by way of recourse to recover their investment.

Simultaneously, Bitcoin mining went from being an inexpensive operation achievable from a personal computer to being an industrial undertaking requiring vast amounts of hardware and energy. In the background, politicians and world governments watched and waited, unsure about exactly how to control, far less legislate this new species of digital currency.

This book is therefore the product of this journey into the confusing world of Bitcoin and Satoshi Nakamoto. The intention is to tell the Bitcoin story it in a way that is relatable to normal people—anyone with just a passing interest in one of the world's most significant inventions. Still, I fully accept that this is the tech world we're talking about, and as much as the objective was to distil the most technical aspects of the story to the bare minimum: blockchains, nodes, miners, protocols, etc., a degree of tech-speak must be employed.

Thankfully though, far above all of the technology surrounding Bitcoin towers a much more relatable and fundamental truth that wasn't immediately obvious. What I came to realize over time was that the narrative of Bitcoin's short fifteen years of life is a modern morality tale playing out before our eyes. Greed, betrayal, hunger for power, and good versus evil: all of these primal forces are present—just as they have been in almost every famous story ever told—from the Bible to Shakespeare to *Harry Potter*, the contents of which can teach us a thing or two about the nuances of human nature.

Where the Bitcoin story differs from classic books is that it exists in an era where the skewing of identity and the bending of reality, online and elsewhere, has become de-rigueur. To that extent, it is difficult to look at the Bitcoin narrative through the traditional lenses of fact or fiction, or even good and bad. Instead, Bitcoin, and the players in it, operate in the murky margins where truth and virtue are hard to identify at all, far less hold up to traditional means of scrutiny. Faced with this kind of challenge, all we can do is try to make the story fit within the world we recognize.

My introduction to this weird netherworld of Bitcoin came about by near accident. I was one of the many for whom Bitcoin, blockchain technology (the foundation system on which Bitcoin runs), and the concept of cryptocurrency in general was a closed book.

Like many of a certain age—a "boomer" in cryptocurrency parlance is what people like me are called—I suppose I saw it as a shady world into which I had no real need to venture either. I had a bank account and was fine with phone-based banking apps to make my transactions easier. That was enough technology. I saw no need for anything else. However, during a book project I began working on in 2019, my outlook changed when I was forced into a sink or swim position, whereby I either had to learn about Bitcoin in a hurry in order to receive payment for some work, or not get paid at all. Not being especially keen on the latter, at the age of fifty I descended into the confusing world of Bitcoin with little more than Google as my point of entry.

After a couple of days trying to figure out how to sign up to a cryptocurrency exchange, and then several more days trying to figure out how to convert bitcoin to dollars and then dollars into pounds sterling, I was both exhausted and bewildered.

As I read more about the subject on the various Reddit forums and watched select interviews online on the huge array of Bitcoin-related channels, the vituperation and aggressive territorialism quickly became apparent. Some Reddit forums seemed to exist for no other reason than to promote one side of the Bitcoin debate, while at the same time trashing the credentials of potential candidates for the Satoshi mantle. Of course, I wanted to understand what or who was propelling the toxic environment that shrouded the Bitcoin world. To an outsider like I was, it all seemed so disproportionately divisive. With the emergence of two new symbols to accompany the original Bitcoin ticker symbol (the symbol that identifies a cryptocurrency on an exchange), when the Bitcoin network split via hard "forks" (where a new chain is created in the bigger blockchain) in 2017 (to Bitcoin Cash—BCH) and 2018 (from BCH to Bitcoin SV—BSV), regular people could have been forgiven for not knowing what the word "Bitcoin" actually referred to, given that there were now three main variants: BTC, BCH, and BSV, all of which had their own values, technical ideologies, and vocal devotees, albeit that neither of the latter two have come close to matching BTC's value. Basically, it appeared as if Bitcoin was like the confluence of several fanatical religions where contrasting views were simply not tolerated. In fact, it was worse than that. It was actual civil war.

But why?

Surely, it wasn't just a case of rival factions arguing about events from fifteen years prior? I started to wonder whether much more was at stake where the provenance of Bitcoin was concerned. There was—and I needed to separate the signal from the noise.

On a simplistic level, I suppose it stood to reason that an invention with the potential for such profound impact on the future of mankind would draw some potentially dark artists into the arena. Recent history is full of anarchist types who have sought to hide their activities from the prying eyes of governments by creating currencies to rival the established standards. Some probably saw Bitcoin as merely the next opportunity of this kind, especially given that it arrived, coincidentally some say, at the epicenter of a global financial crisis when peoples' trust for traditional financial institutions was at an all-time low. At the same time, financial institutions like banks, PayPal, and credit card companies must have viewed Bitcoin as a terminal threat. Why would anyone use PayPal or a credit card and incur hefty fees if Bitcoin could be used at a fraction of the price?

I started to wonder if what made Bitcoin so threatening was that it *was* different from everything that came before. Let's be clear. At no point was Bitcoin presented as a means of purchasing illegal goods anonymously and avoiding tax. Indeed, the entire ledger system on which Bitcoin was based made the act of purchasing illegal goods traceable, and therefore deeply perilous. If anything, rather than facilitating tax evasion, Bitcoin made the practice of paying tax easier and more transparent.

Bitcoin really was a white knight that stood its ground to the too-many people who wanted to commit crime and the too-many organizations whose business models relied on charging fees. Viewed like this, it was easy to see how the dynamics within the Bitcoin world would be turbulent and toxic.

My next more serious entry into the Bitcoin business came about as a result of some email communication with a PR company in London called Lightning Sharks, who I'd later discover operate from a nondescript second floor office in Golden Square, Soho.

Initially, I merely wanted to ask if Canadian billionaire Calvin Ayre, for whom the company appeared to conduct PR work in conjunction with the website *CoinGeek*, would consider endorsing an experimental NFT book project of mine soon to be launching on the Bitcoin blockchain. As a major player in the Bitcoin world, I knew all too well how much value his endorsement would carry. If I wanted these NFTs to sell out quickly, I knew that Ayre's seal of approval would help. I also knew that Ayre was a major backer of the original Bitcoin protocol—BSV—devised by Satoshi Nakamoto, and had a business relationship with the man who appeared to be behind the pseudonym who invented it, an Australian scientist named Craig Steven Wright. As to the extent and nature of this relationship, I was still in the dark. I wanted to know more. And soon I would.

CHAPTER **ONE**

Mayfair

April 8th, 2022

I had no idea what to expect from Calvin Ayre in person. I hadn't met any billionaires. The most recent article I'd read about him, in the *Daily Mail*, had him pictured at Dumfries House, one of the homes belonging to Charles, now King of England, in an article about a joint venture to build new homes on the Caribbean island of Barbuda in the aftermath of Hurricane Irma in 2017.

The arrangement was that I was to meet him and other members of the Lightning Sharks team at a restaurant in Central London. "Come down and have lunch. We have a couple of ideas to discuss," I was told.

Getting to London by train from Scotland in time was going to be difficult, as I knew I'd have very little leeway to get across the city when I arrived at Kings Cross. Halfway through the six-hour train journey, I received another email from my Lightning Sharks contact.

"Calvin has been working in Europe all week. He's bored and wants to relax today. Can you meet us at a private address instead?" it said.

"No problem," I replied, relieved that I no longer had to rush to make a firm restaurant booking.

I was given a postcode with the instruction to press the intercom at the agreed time. I got off the train, jumped onto the underground on the Victoria line, and emerged into the West End, springtime sunlight.

Using Google maps, I walked half a mile from the tube station and turned right down a quiet street with austere but clearly high-end terraced residential properties on one side and a couple of low-key restaurants on the other. I easily found the property, walked up the three steps outside, and rang the intercom on which there was no name. Taxis and the occasional fast food delivery motorcycle whizzed behind me as I stood waiting to be buzzed in.

After a minute or two, a young-sounding female's voice answered. I said my name and waited. Shortly afterwards, the heavy, black door swung open and I walked into a large, round hallway. Freshly cut flowers adorned the side tables. The house's name hung on a cute driftwood sign in an alcove on the left. Expensive furniture was all around and an ornate chandelier hung above us. It was as if I'd walked through a portal into another dimension. The house exuded wealth.

It was the kind of home where you remove your shoes and maybe even your feet, and I wasn't sure if I should take off mine. The young lady who'd answered the intercom introduced herself, and then my Lightning Sharks contact appeared from up the hallway to receive me. We hugged in a kind of awkward man-embrace—the kind that you do when you've never met but have been emailing for two weeks. I asked about the shoes and the suggestion was waved away with a friendly hand gesture.

I followed my contact through a long passageway with a large stairway leading both upwards and downwards off to the left, and into a dining room that had a long table laid out with nice food and a selection of drinks, as if for a party. Out the window to the rear I could see what looked like a large outdoor entertaining area, guarded by a high wall to the west. As I stood staring at the array of food, in the near distance I could hear music throbbing. I was offered a drink. I asked for sparkling water. I turned right into the next room, a long, ornate sitting room with a grand piano in the center and a long, velvet sofa at the far end, and there I saw my host in front of me.

I'd anticipated a few eventualities in the lead up to this revised meeting, but to find Calvin Ayre adorned in a kilt down below with a white vest on top was not one of them. Whether this Scottish gesture was in my honor I had no idea, but I took it that way anyway.

For his sixty years, the man looked undeniably fit and healthy on first sight. I noticed that his upper arms, one of which was tattooed with what looked like Japanese symbols, were toned in a way that suggested this was a guy who worked out. His hair, silver-grey and closely cropped at the sides, was youthfully slicked back on top, creating a kind of straightedge look. He had a friendly smile and blue eyes that scanned faces and logged details.

Calvin Ayre was holding a glass of what looked like champagne in one hand and was jiving to the music quite stylishly. Two exotic girls danced by his side as the music pumped. One looked South American, the other perhaps Thai, although we were never formally introduced. Both looked very happy to be there. I was a little more circumspect. This was not the business meeting I had expected. Regardless, I strode toward my billionaire host and extended my hand as my Lightning Sharks contact introduced me as "the writer we talked about." I gripped Ayre's hand tight and stared into the blacks of his eyes as they, in turn, intimately scanned the person in front of them and stored a digital receipt in their owner's brain.

"Good to see the kilt," I said. "What's underneath it?" I added, totally deadpan.

I knew that this comment could have gone down a couple of ways with someone whose sense of humor I didn't know at all. There was a momentary pause as the cheeky question, perhaps delayed momentarily by the numbing effects of alcohol, landed. To my relief, Ayre's head flew back as he laughed heartily. As he did, I could smell the champagne when he exhaled. Looking at the bottle on the drinks trolley beside us, I could see it was vintage and expensive.

"Ya, I've got Scottish ancestors you know. I'm a descendant of Robert the Bruce," he told me, in a pronounced, clipped Canadian accent. "And there's nothing underneath the kilt," he added, belly-laughing again. "Do you want to see?"

I took his word for it, and with ice broken somewhat, we began talking in an attempt to quickly get each other's measure.

Calvin Ayre told me again about his fondness for Scotland and explained how, because of the obvious name similarity, he and his company, Bodog, had sponsored the unfashionable Scottish soccer team Ayr United during the domestic season of 2011/2012—partly for fun, and partly in an attempt to build the small club's brand in the Asian market. Fittingly, topless painted girls modelled the new shirts carrying the company name for that season at the official launch.

"Did you consider just buying the team outright?" I asked him.

"No, not really," Ayre said. "We had some fun while we were involved though and I loved going up there."

As we got to know each other, it became clear that this party I'd just joined had been going for a while. My friendly host was nicely lubricated and I wasn't sure whether this state would make our conversations easier or otherwise. I had no idea how to play the man at all.

One of the concerns I had prior to the meeting was that my previous project had been with the late tech maverick John McAfee, with whom Ayre had had a very nasty and public spat on Twitter in 2019. I knew they hadn't liked each other, for a variety reasons, and I was keen to clear the air and make it known that, as much as I'd worked with McAfee, I neither agreed with everything he said nor endorsed all of his actions. Basically, I wanted to get ahead of it and to play it all down.

"John was fucking rude," Ayre said, when the subject inevitably came up. "The man was a prick."

"I hear you. I don't want your opinion of me in any way colored by anyone I've worked with," I explained. "It's not my job to judge, just to tell the story. And anyway, he's dead."

I suggested that we bury the infamous Twitter argument right there and then by raising a glass to McAfee. Initially, Ayre didn't look too enthused by the idea.

"Come on. Let's put it all in the past," I urged, pushing my glass into the center of the three of us, as if to invite others to do the same. With that, my contact looked at Ayre with an expression of encouragement and a gesture that said, "Why not?" The three of us raised a toast to John McAfee in Calvin Ayre's sitting room. Meanwhile, a young lady appeared, offering to open more bottles of champagne.

"I'm sorry about this," my contact whispered in my ear as the host peeled away and danced to the next song—"Rhythm Is a Dancer" by Snap! as I recall.

"We can organize a proper meet soon. We'll obviously pay your expenses…" he said.

"No, I'm actually okay with this as it is," I replied. "I think this might even be a better way to meet than what we had planned."

At this point, however, I had to make a decision whether to stick with the sparkling water or to go along with the mood and have a real drink. Part of me was aware that I had to be back at London's King Cross station at 5:30 p.m. later that afternoon for the return train home. I had no change of clothes and no hotel booked. I *had* to be on that train.

However, thinking I could compromise and go with the mood a little, and also sensing that it all might be some kind of personality test, I agreed to a glass of champagne when I was next offered a refill. Any suggestion of lunch, food, of which there was plenty, just melted away.

I should say that at this initial point of contact, I knew as much or as little about the history of Bitcoin as far as how it intertwined with the identity of Satoshi Nakamoto as the next person. I'd read mainstream news articles and suppose, if I'm being truthful, took most of the information I found there as wrote because I didn't have time or the need to do anything else. However, as I researched the subject more deeply, I kept seeing the same names crop up.

Craig Steven Wright was the one I had seen most often, and the reason I was seeing it was twofold. Firstly, back in 2015, Wright had been crudely "outed" against his will by two publications, *WIRED* and *Gizmodo*, in salacious articles proclaiming that he was the person behind the mysterious Satoshi Nakamoto pseudonym—the man who invented Bitcoin and had published the celebrated and revolutionary white paper on the subject in late 2008.

Predictably, the articles opened a Pandora's box of information and associated discussion that has never been closed since. In addition to shining a light on private emails between Craig Wright and his US-based friend David Kleiman that appeared to indicate that the two were discussing and perhaps even collaborating on the Bitcoin white paper, also laid bare was communication between Wright, his lawyer, and the Australian Taxation Office that made it appear as if the tax office were aware of Wright's role in the creation of Bitcoin. Looking at the leaked information on face value—and face value is admittedly just one dimension by which to view information in today's world—it was hard to argue with the suggestion that Wright was indeed the creator of Bitcoin.

Inevitably, he wasn't alone. Craig Wright was far from the first Satoshi Nakamoto candidate that had been offered up to the world. But even still, the *WIRED* and *Gizmodo* articles (both of which were quickly retracted) contained revelations that were hard to dismiss, even for Wright's most ardent critics.

From a credibility perspective, the magazines' claims—assertions that were gleaned from lengthy, parallel investigations—brought to light specific details and timelines relating to Wright's expertise, personality, and background that appeared to align in a way that nobody else's had. Because of this perception credibility, Wright's public unmasking grabbed the headlines in a way that nothing else previously had or would since. The story was mainstream news that few could avoid and even those with little prior interest in Bitcoin could well have read the material and come to the conclusion that, for all that the evidence was a complicated rabbit hole of claims and counter claims, Wright, in the absence of a more convincing candidate, was probably Satoshi Nakamoto.

The second reason Craig Wright had stayed on my radar was that in 2021, Wright had been one half of a high profile $66 billion dollar, at its height, lawsuit in the state of Florida, the purpose of which was to establish *not* whether Wright was in fact Satoshi Nakamoto (that "truth" was implied from the outset), but whether the other participant in the lawsuit, the estate of a late American computer programmer and former friend of Wright's, Dave Kleiman, was legally part of a partnership with Wright related to the invention of Bitcoin, and therefore entitled to associated proceeds and intellectual property rights.

It was an important case that only ever came to court *because* of Wright's "outing" six years prior. Indeed, many conclude that

Wright was unmasked simply so that he could later be sued by Dave Kleiman's brother, Ira, who was rumored to have been communicating at best, scheming at worst, either directly or indirectly, with the Australian Taxation Office, the magazine journalists, and other individuals who were vying to flush out Craig Wright into the public glare. Obviously, because of the significance of the case and the financial stakes in play, Satoshi Nakamoto and Bitcoin were again mainstream news because of the Kleiman trial.

In late 2021, Wright emerged from the lawsuit as the victor, albeit that he did so with a caveat, when a jury ruled in his favor on six of seven counts on one hand, while at the same time ordering him to pay a co-plaintiff in the case, W&K Info Defense Research LLC, a company that Kleiman had owned a 25% stake in, $100 million dollars.

Not only was this number insignificant in the wider context of the case's financial scope, a notable twist was that it was Wright's ex-wife Lynn who owned the other 75 percent share of that same company. The net result was that the same proportion of the money Wright was ordered to pay—$75 million dollars—would ultimately find its way back to his ex-wife, with whom he remains on friendly terms.

Not to downplay the financial implications of Wright vs. Kleiman in any way, but it seemed that the most significant aspects of the case's outcome was that the ruling in Wright's favor lifted much of the cloud of doubt and suspicion that had cloaked him since the WIRED and Gizmodo articles landed in October of 2015. And there had been plenty of opposition.

Ever since he'd been unmasked against his will in late 2015, there had been a shadowy and highly toxic campaign to discredit Wright and his work. In a strange way, the magazine articles that had initially tried to lend credibility to the idea that Wright was Satoshi had ultimately managed to achieve precisely the opposite.

Even the news outlets themselves, perhaps fearing they'd been duped, panicked. Before long it appeared as if they were questioning their own claims and had apparently lost all confidence in their own sources—assuming they even knew who those sources were. They even went as far as to issue retractions to save face, after suggestions surfaced that Wright was in fact a scammer at the center of an elaborate fraud concocted to out himself.

Suspicion about Wright only intensified thereafter. "Faketoshi," as he became known as in Bitcoin circles—all despite a polished, carefully curated media exercise intended to remove all doubt.

The culmination of the attempt to prove Wright was Satoshi was, ironically, the most damaging event of all. Indeed, instead of a now infamous 2016 interview with the BBC and an accompanying proof exercise being the slam-dunk that answered all remaining questions about the identity of Satoshi Nakamoto, the clumsy event that pushed a clearly traumatized Craig Wright far outside his comfort zone merely invited more skepticism and criticism. Some of the motivation behind the dislike for the man was clearly personal. Wright reputedly suffers from a combination of autism and Asperger's Syndrome and has an intolerant and abrasive house-style that doesn't necessarily endear him to either the press or his detractors. Furthermore, in a world where people crave glamor wherever they look, there was nothing whatsoever sexy about Satoshi Nakamoto being an unknown forty-five-year-old Australian computer scientist with an anti-social attitude. People will never ever match up to myths, but Craig Wright was the Satoshi nobody wanted.

Much more of the animosity seemed to be motivated by jealousy and greed, perhaps fueled by the fact that Satoshi Nakamoto had mined and held significant reserves (in excess of one million coins, some reports said) of bitcoin—more than enough to wield influence upon the market price if they were ever to dump/sell the holdings and more than enough to make Wright one of the world's richest men.

There was a further tsunami of opposition to Wright that stemmed from fundamental disagreements about how Bitcoin should function going forward in a technical sense. Again, many wanted Bitcoin to be the force for good that Satoshi championed, where cheap, fast transactions could transform the lives of people and businesses worldwide, especially in third world countries. Equally, others clearly saw Bitcoin as an opportunity to commit dark acts involving anonymous money that could be hidden from governments. To this extent, Bitcoin really was a tug-of-war between good and evil, and Satoshi was in the middle, being pulled in either direction.

Consequently, the possibility of Craig Wright being Satoshi Nakamoto, and all the power, platform, and cultural responsibility that accompanied such a role, was and still is an unpalatable proposition for many in the world of not just Bitcoin, but also consumer finance, and even perhaps, top level politics. As a result, his haters—and there were many—would seemingly do anything to discredit, silence, or in an ideal world, crush him and his ideas.

An old adage, often wrongly credited to Sun Tzu's *The Art of War*, holds that if you wait by the riverbank long enough, the bodies of your enemies will eventually float by. That's as good a metaphor as any for how Craig Wright must have felt when the verdict in the Kleiman trial was delivered in March 2022.

Despite winning the case, in 2022 Craig Wright was as divisive as he'd been in 2015 among Bitcoin devotees, arguably much more so. But instead of shrinking away in the aftermath of some startling revelations at trial about his early work with Bitcoin, Wright seemed emboldened and determined to continue on the offensive. Not only was he now taking swipes at his detractors by engaging on Twitter with trademark withering retorts, offering more interviews, and appearing at conferences as the creator of Bitcoin, but he was also getting litigious and suing his critics in a number of court cases in various jurisdictions in the aftermath of his significant win in Florida.

Anyone could see that it was a war, and the stakes were only getting higher. Not only was Craig Wright fortified by lawsuit success, but he also appeared to be fighting fire with fire with his Bitcoin enemies as far as financial backing was concerned. To that end, looming in the background to support Wright was Calvin Ayre.

Precisely how Ayre fit into the bigger Bitcoin picture I wasn't totally sure, but I was aware he somehow did and was very much in the same orbit as people like Wright. Furthermore, Ayre owned the website *CoinGeek*, which even I could see took a very strong position when it came to publicizing the assertion that Wright is Satoshi Nakamoto. Beyond that, I knew that Ayre had several homes but seemed to live primarily in the Caribbean and that he'd made his fortune in the sports betting industry in Canada. Indeed, by the mid 2000s, his company Bodog, a name chosen specifically so that it could be memorable and transferable across a variety of business platforms, was turning over vast sums of money as the online gambling industry exploded.

In parallel, Ayre, projecting a playful bad-boy-who-liked-to-have-a-good-time image synonymous with a certain type of lifestyle—yachts, fast cars, scantily clad women, and seemingly endless parties presided over by armed bodyguards—became something of a celebrity himself by appearing on shows like MTV's *Cribs* and VH1's *Fabulous Life of...* Simultaneously, his name started appearing on lists such as *People* magazine's "40 hottest bachelors" and his photogenic face on the cover of *Forbes*' Billionaires issue.

But as much as Ayre's lifestyle might have looked frivolous and clichéd, there was considerable business acumen behind the playboy mask. Ayre was a master at identifying an emerging market and he knew how to capitalize when he entered one. This was a man who'd reputedly sold fruit from a truck parked by the side of the highway when he was a teenager, after all. Ayre was never averse to the idea of industrious endeavor. Indeed, Bodog had been created on the back of a simple newspaper article Ayre had read in 1992 about the advent of telephone betting in the Caribbean.

Attention piqued and seed of inspiration sown, from there he taught himself network design from manuals and created software support which he then licensed to online casinos before realizing that there was way more money in actually *being* the house than propping it up. He launched his own gambling operation in 1996 and never looked back.

Once in the market, Ayre knew how to build and deliver a killer brand. In a visionary marketing move that he claimed was simply based on his own day-to-day reality, Ayre made sure that the company played heavily on an idea he called "the Bodog lifestyle," which, in truth, was just Ayre's own daily antics projected onto the world by his company image and slick advertising. Via Ayre's flamboyant persona, Bodog was basically saying to its online customers, "You can have this too." And it worked, because customers flooded in. And since the house always wins in the gambling business, significant revenues followed. Bodog continued flying high and Ayre was extending his influence and brand into online poker, launching *Calvin Ayre Wildcard Poker* on Fox Sports. Even when police raided the after after-party of the first season finale in Costa Rica because they mistakenly believed illegal gambling to be taking place, Ayre didn't blink—quite the reverse. Law enforcement's involvement was a gift received with open arms. Ayre used the publicity to spin the Bodog brand harder. In turn, he became the number one gambling mogul for a time.

The Unlawful Internet Gambling Enforcement Act of 2006 essentially ended Bodog's activities in the US, however. US authorities were going around arresting high profile executives across the online gambling world at the time and Calvin Ayre had no desire to be one of them, so he cut his losses and sold the US aspect of his company to the Morris Mohawk Gaming Group in Quebec, bowing out of the online gambling world altogether, although he retained ownership of the branding and the Bodog domain.

Despite having relinquished involvement in the US facing aspect of Bodog, Ayre continued to prosper, focusing instead on overseas initiatives and his Calvin Ayre Foundation that had been established in 2005 and channeled considerable philanthropic energy in areas such as animal welfare, education for the disadvantaged, and protection of the environment. By 2010, Ayre could seemingly do no wrong. Despite his extrovert image, he had become extremely credible as both a generous philanthropist and shrewd business head.

In 2012 however, the Ayre roof caved in spectacularly. He and three other company employees were indicted by the US Attorney for Maryland, accused of illegal gambling and money laundering in contravention of the Unlawful Internet Gambling Enforcement Act that had come into effect in 2006. These were retrospective charges relating to their activities *prior* to the passage of the act itself. Regardless, the Bodog.com domain was seized. It seemed like the party was over.

As a younger man, Ayre, having graduated with a bachelor's degree in sciences from the University of Waterloo, was no stranger to either the entrepreneur spirit or the occasional alleged controversy. Infamously, his father Ken, a pig farmer in Lloydminster, Saskatchewan, was convicted of smuggling marijuana from Jamaica to Canada in 1987 and was sentenced to four years in jail for his troubles. Calvin, just twenty-six at the time, played no part in the proceedings whatsoever, but because he was being pursued by a Vancouver-based journalist at the time who openly confessed to being anti-online gambling and had written several articles questioning Ayre's motives, later found himself being falsely implicated.

In 1991, in a separate incident, Ayre, while working for a medical supply company, made a naive administrative law error relating to the filing of inside share reports (*not* insider trading as has been falsely reported online). Six years after the company went under, the BC Securities Commission came after Ayre, and the upshot was that, because he was already snowed under with his gaming company activities, he handed the responsibility off to his lawyers and ultimately agreed to a fine of $10,000 and was banished from the Vancouver Stock Exchange for twenty years.

Faced with these new and more serious legal issues in 2012, Ayre did not accede to the US government pressure, instead preferring to spin the accusation as simply "abuse of the US criminal justice system for the commercial gain of large US corporations." Ayre strategically played the victim, and, in doing so, he had a point. Although the vast majority of Bodog's customer base had been in the US, it was an online company operating not on US land from bricks and mortar premises but instead from somewhere out there in the ether. Furthermore, given that Ayre wasn't an American citizen and Bodog had no physical assets in the US that could be seized, Ayre seemed to have a reasonable argument. Nevertheless, the indictment heralded a battle over a legal grey area that Ayre was more than happy to take his chances on winning.

As strong as his stance was, the indictment in Maryland, aside from torpedoing his business activities for a while, would signal the beginning of a frustrating five-year-long fight with the US authorities to clear his name, all of which Ayre conducted from his homes in Antigua and Canada, out of the reach of US jurisdiction and insulated from spiraling legal costs by his billionaire fortune.

Clear his name he did. In July of 2017, the US dropped the charges against Calvin Ayre and Bodog after Ayre pled guilty to a much lesser misdemeanor charge and admitted to an accessory "after the fact" charge relating to the "transmission of gambling information." He was sentenced to one year of unsupervised probation and paid a $500,000 fine.

There was to be a strange twist a few months later however when the Democracy Institute think tank published what amounted to a damning report on how Ayre and his case had been handled. The report claimed that US law enforcement officials had been trying to intimidate Ayre years prior to the filing of his indictment. Not only that, the report further suggested that prosecutors had attempted to contact Ayre covertly through third parties, all with a view to "encourage" Ayre to make a $350 million dollar payment to the US Treasury—presumably to make his problems go away.

In the end, a World Trade Organization ruling represented vindication for Ayre and embarrassment for US authorities, when it was ruled that America was in violation of its obligations under its GATS schedule by enforcing laws associated with the Illegal Gambling Business Act. After five years of purgatory, by the end of 2107 Ayre was free to travel freely and explore the next phase of his entrepreneurial career.

The twin islands government said in a statement, "In light of the WTO ruling in Antigua and Barbuda's favor, prosecutions by the United States of licensed gaming entities and their principals in Antigua and Barbuda, such as Calvin Ayre, are completely contrary to binding international agreements. In this context, Calvin Ayre and all other Antigua and Barbuda licensed gaming operators, who were indicted in the United States on Internet Gaming charges, are victims not culprits."

Knowing vaguely about Ayre's interest in Bitcoin and connection to Wright and not being totally sure what we were there to discuss, I decided to formalize the conversation a little while the going remained good, in the hope of getting some clarity on whether there was a book project to discuss.

"Why are you in this?" I asked him—"this," meaning Bitcoin.

"I suppose I see this is my legacy," he told me. "I want to show the world that I'm not the person they think I am. I want to eclipse any indiscretions in my past by showing that I can help people and do good in the world," he added.

"So are you looking to engage someone to co-write your auto-biography?" I asked.

"No, that's not it. We're considering producing a book about the real history of Bitcoin and how the whole thing is this big scam," Ayre replied.

"How do you mean it's a scam?" I asked.

"There is only one Bitcoin. BSV," Ayre said. "Everything else, BTC for example, is a fraud. How much do you know about BSV?" he added, referring to the variant of Bitcoin that had been restored in 2018 to perpetuate Satoshi Nakamoto's original protocol as set out by his 2008 white paper.

"Well, I know that it scales where others don't," I said—that was about all I knew.

Ayre's eyes widened and he then broke into a broad smile.

"It scales. Yes!" he yelled, throwing his arms to the sky.

"Ya, this guy knows his stuff," he added, gesturing for the attention of his colleague beside me, who by this point had also submitted to the party mood and was drinking champagne.

"What's your connection to Craig Wright though?" I asked.

This question coincided with a sudden, gaping silence that reminded me of a scene in the 1980s movie *An American Werewolf in London* when two American tourists walk into a remote pub on the Yorkshire moors, point to a pentangle on the wall scrawled in blood and ask, "What's that star symbol on the wall for?"

"Craig was fucking drowning. I pulled him out of the swimming pool and dumped him on the side. We saved Craig Wright. We saved Bitcoin," Ayre told me very seriously.

I was genuinely shocked at how earnest my host had become, even though what he was saying was clearly figurative and just a little cryptic.

In what sense was Craig Wright drowning?

How was Bitcoin saved? I thought to myself.

Whatever the answers were, it was clear that Ayre was describing a situation the gravity of which I had grossly underestimated.

"Someone needs to tell this story," Ayre said. "But I'm warning you, they'll come for you too if you do," he added a little ominously.

"What do you mean?" I asked. "And who's 'they'?" I added.

"The trolls online, for a start. Any book you write could get shut down too," he told me.

Ayre went on to explain how he believed that nefarious forces—perhaps even three letter agencies—in the US and beyond were plotting against BSV and Craig Wright. "You won't believe how deep this stuff runs," he told me.

As if to qualify this in language I'd understand, he also told me about a previous book that had been written entitled *Behind the Mask: Craig Wright and the Battle for Bitcoin* that was co-written by two eminent Reuter's journalists Byron Kaye and Jeremy Wagstaff. The book had a masked image of Craig Wright's face on the cover and reputedly contained first-hand interviews with Wright and others in his immediate world and had been scheduled for publication in January of 2020 via a small Australian imprint called Affirm Press.

Then, out of nowhere, everything went quiet. The book was never published and no explanation was given as to why not. The two co-authors have refused to offer any comment since. Further information about what happened to the book and the rights to the material is conspicuous by its absence online. The book, one that Craig Wright himself had apparently pre-ordered, just vanished. Whatever was behind the mask, it seemed as if somebody wanted it to stay there.

"It was caught and killed," Ayre explained, using an expression that describes how a media outlet uses a subtle technique involving a non-disclosure agreement to prevent an individual revealing information about a third party. The rights are purchased—"the catch"—and then the information is never published—"the kill."

"By whom, and why?" I asked, fully aware that books get cancelled all the time with no explanation from their publishers.

"We don't know," he told me. "But we have some ideas," he added.

"These are reputable high-profile writers at major publications. Why won't they explain what happened?" I asked.

"They must have been paid off," Ayre said. "Or threatened."

As extreme and as unproven as Ayre's suggestions were, I couldn't deny that I was getting a stronger sense of the seriousness of the Bitcoin world. Indeed, if Ayre's assertion about this Bitcoin book was true, this was not just some trivial high school argument being conducted on places like Reddit by a bunch of basement trolls out to make a quick buck. No, this was serious business, with big picture consequences. Craig Wright, if he was indeed Satoshi Nakamoto, was a pariah. Not only that, from where I was sitting it appeared as if his original Bitcoin protocol, BSV, was clearly in someone's crosshairs along with seemingly anyone attached to it. At the risk of sounding like Philip Marlow, I had to ask myself if I had the stomach to find out why.

"If I was to undertake a project like this, I'd need access to everybody," I said. "And that includes Craig Wright."

"Well, the next step might be for you to come down and meet Craig," my contact suggested. "We'll take care of everything, your expenses."

"Dragged him from the pool, dumped him on the side soaking wet. Ha!" Ayre chimed in again. "But ya—you can meet Craig. We'll organize that."

"I'll leave it to you to set it up," I said.

As the glasses of champagne started morphing into fishbowls of rum, things started getting a little hazy. Conversations were being repeated and the subjects only became more eclectic. One minute we were debating the merits of Phil Collins's solo career versus his Genesis years. Then we started talking about the benefits of Ayahuasca, a South American psychoactive drink potion common to shamanic spiritual medicine, and Ayre even suggested we all go on a retreat together in "a year or so."

For no obvious reason, I was then offered a tour of the house by my Lightning Sharks contact. It was an undeniably fabulous property on several levels, with a dizzying array of rooms not unlike a boutique five-star hotel. As we arrived in a basement spa, with hot tubs, private treatment areas, saunas, and steam rooms, my contact pointed toward the seductively lit swimming pool against the far wall.

"The party might move down here later," I was told.

I think I knew what that meant and was relieved to note that I had just one hour and forty-five minutes to get across town to King's Cross. We returned to the sitting room, where the drinking and dancing had continued in our absence, and I thanked Ayre for his hospitality and the opportunity to talk in person.

I left the house, walked outside into the cool afternoon air not really knowing exactly what the next steps might be. It seemed like we had a good personal understanding and I couldn't deny that I found his relentless positivity to be highly infectious. Furthermore, it felt like there might actually be an interesting project to discuss. How it might come together and under what terms was less clear.

My chaperone for the day suggested that we have a quick beer somewhere on my way to the station. Kind of a debrief, he said. We found a Japanese restaurant near Savile Row that he knew, went upstairs to a deserted rooftop bar where bored looking staff prepared for the evening dinner service. We ordered an Asahi beer each and sat looking out over Mayfair, going through the day's events. As we talked about subjects ranging from Bitcoin to how we survived the pandemic, time ebbed away. Suddenly, in a moment of panic, I realized that I didn't have as much time as I thought to catch the train. Plus, it was Friday rush hour. I had to move.

I ran downstairs and out into the street. There were no taxis to be seen. Finally, one appeared, and I told the driver where to go and to be quick about it. "I'll do my best, mate," he said. "But traffic's nuts tonight. I'll get you so far but you might be quicker to get out and run."

He was right. As we reached Euston Underpass on the A501 with my train departing in six minutes, all I could see was bumper-to-bumper traffic stretching far into the distance. "Forget the fare, mate," the driver said. "Just go."

With that I got out and ran along Euston Road, new shoes gnawing into my feet with every step, until I arrived breathless at platform one where I was relieved to see the train still there. I climbed aboard, found my reserved seat, and slumped down.

On the train home, as the guy diagonally opposite removed, studied, and replaced his false teeth every once in a while, I pondered the day's events with the taste of fine Caribbean rum still to the fore, all the time considering what might play out next and whether I wanted it to play out at all given some of the things I'd been told about the Bitcoin world.

I wouldn't have long to wait. Early the next morning, there was an email waiting from Ayre when I woke up with a subject line that read, "So do you still want the gig?"

Before responding, I wanted to give serious thought to what "the gig" might actually entail.

As I deliberated, I acknowledged to myself that the idea of writing about Craig Wright's role in Bitcoin certainly did appeal. The subject had existed outside my comfort zone for so long and such situations are appealing. Not just that, it was clear that with various court cases looming involving Craig Wright, we were at a critical moment in Bitcoin's trajectory where telling the inside story might indeed have widespread appeal.

Thinking about what such a project might look like, my only two concerns were access and objectivity—and how those two intertwined in this instance or even if they did at all.

It was already clear that I would get access to everyone who believed—and preached publicly—that Craig Wright is Satoshi Nakamoto. However, that was only one side of the story. To present the full and even-handed picture, it was necessary to get the perspective of some of the Craig Wright deniers, and perhaps, the active haters. This was the kind of objectivity I needed, and I wasn't totally sure how, in such a fiercely divisive world, I was going to get it.

"Of course!" I replied to the email, leaving the ball firmly in Ayre's court as far as where the conversation went next.

He quickly fired back asking what I thought a book on the subject might look like and it was then that I explained how important I thought it was to present the story in such a way that not only looked at events objectively, but also expressed the gravity of Bitcoin's potential role in the world going forward, all of which was there to see for anyone who cared to read Satoshi's white paper. As I thought about it more, I really did start seeing

Bitcoin in the same context as the invention of the wheel. Equally, I saw Satoshi Nakamoto in the same light as great pioneers from history like Edison, Baird, or Alan Turing.

After a bit more to and fro, it was agreed that I'd be given access to everyone I wanted in Craig Wright's orbit, including Wright himself. I should say that I felt as if I had to push for this particular aspect. Albeit subtle, I did feel a degree of resistance to this idea.

"Craig is always so busy," I was told. "But don't worry, we'll set up a meeting in Surrey sometime down the line in the summer."

As it turned out, I wouldn't have long to wait for plans to concretize. Arrangements moved at real pace. It was intoxicating to see how quickly people like Calvin Ayre could mobilize resources.

Within a few days I'd received a lengthy NDA to sign. A day or two later, an invite with a plus-one for a social event in London at which, I was told, Craig Wright would appear. Curious about the possibility of meeting Wright in person, I made plans for the trip to London. As I did so, I felt as if I was being ushered into an inner world.

A few days prior to the event I was emailed about a meeting scheduled to take place at Calvin Ayre's house in the afternoon before the party at which Wright and another key player in the Bitcoin and blockchain world, Stefan Matthews, would be in attendance.

I quickly read up about Matthews and could see that he was an experienced and highly respected Australian entrepreneur who'd operated at boardroom levels in the betting industry prior to coming on-board with Craig Wright circles officially in 2015. What his actual role was now, I wasn't totally sure. Nevertheless, I was keen to meet him.

On the designated date, I climbed the steps to Ayre's house in London and rang the entry panel once again with the events of a month prior still fresh in my mind. After being welcomed inside, however, it was clear that the atmosphere was different. No food and drink were laid out. No dance music pumped. Exotic females were nowhere in sight. Instead, I was directed via a different door into the same room I'd met Ayre in on the first occasion, except this time it was set up for a meeting. People milled around, presumably Lightning Sharks employees, none of whom I'd met before.

Five minutes later, Ayre himself came downstairs, breezed into the room, clearly straight from the shower. This, evidently, was Calvin Ayre 2.0. In place of the kilt and vest was a smart shirt and designer jeans. Under his left arm was a well-worn leather-bound notebook. He looked taller and was clearly in serious business mode. We shook hands again and moved into the private dining room, where Stefan Matthews soon joined us.

Matthews was a different proposition to Ayre altogether. Tall, bald, well built, with a warm smile. Where Ayre could be a little intense and humorless, Matthews was the kind of guy who immediately put you at ease in his company.

As the three of us talked, it became clear to me that there were other differences that were really going to help me. Where Ayre was a dry, stick-to-the-facts type of conversationalist in a business situation, a guy who liked to distil information to its barest form, Matthews was the type who, in his disarming Australian accent, actively relished the art of riffing and storytelling. Indeed, it occurred to me right there and then that, in this capacity as willing, colorful raconteur, anything Stefan Matthews might give me by way of input for a book was likely to be gold dust.

"Craig won't make it until later," Ayre told me. Apparently, he'd been at a blockchain summit in Rabat, Morocco and had missed his flight back to London. "You'll see him tonight though."

I was a little disappointed. I'd been mentally gearing up for my first exposure to the mercurial Wright. Regardless, the three of us sat at the dining room table and Ayre introduced Matthews formally as not just his close friend and colleague, but also as the Executive Chairman of Group, founded in 2015, the Swiss registered blockchain research company with a London office that fronted Craig Wright's day-to-day work in his capacity as Chief Science Officer.

"Don't worry, Stefan, Mark passed the test," Ayre said.

"If you say so," I said, laughing. I assumed he meant that I hadn't been totally put off by the relaxed party antics I had encountered at our first meeting.

Quickly, and to my real surprise, I found myself being briefed on some intimate details relating to recent happenings within the Bitcoin world in addition to confidential details about the future direction of their Bitcoin BSV vision. On one hand, it felt gratifying to be trusted by these two men after such a short time "on the inside" as it were. On another, I felt, perhaps for the first time, the sheer weight of the story I was setting out to tell.

On reflection, what was most striking was the sheer profundity of Ayre's and Matthews's belief. These weren't men who'd taken a speculative punt on the basis that Craig Wright *might* be their man—an accusation that has indeed been levelled at them both frequently. No, these were serious people, each of whom had seen a lot of the business world and had witnessed every nuance of human nature along the way. And yet, Ayre and Matthews were immovable on this subject despite the obvious opposition they faced. They maintained *beyond all possible doubt* that Craig Wright was Satoshi Nakamoto, the creator of Bitcoin.

I can't deny that I found the idea of these two men staking their reputations and possibly their business futures on the "truth" that Craig Wright was Satoshi Nakamoto both admirable and a little unnerving given how much conjecture and downright opposition there was out in the world. In fact, the only thing they appeared to believe in more than Craig Wright being Satoshi Nakamoto was that there were multiple big players in tech and beyond actively trying to silence him.

"This is a conspiracy against Craig," Ayre said. "They are trying to destroy him," he added—echoing what he'd told me at our first meeting.

As much as there were many sound reasons to believe that Wright was indeed Satoshi, even I knew by this early stage in my conversations with these people that there were many out there who were even more sure that Wright was little more than a scam artist who couldn't keep his story straight and who would ultimately be proven a fraud.

Indeed, in the days since our first meeting, I'd done a bit of digging of my own for due-diligence. Before long it became clear to me that there *were* individuals who had dedicated a vast amount of time and effort to this endeavor and who had created blogs and podcasts solely in an attempt to debunk everything Wright related. To that extent, Ayre's assessment of the situation was plausible.

In May of 2022, I sat somewhere in the middle. Whenever I was asked what I thought—and I was a few times—all I could say was that, based on everything I knew, it seemed more likely than not that Craig Wright was Satoshi Nakamoto.

The problem there was that in May 2022 I really didn't know very much at all. I needed to descend a lot deeper into the machine—and to meet Wright myself in person—to be qualified to take any kind of firm position of my own.

May 14th, 2022

My wife and I walked into an exclusive, well-known venue off Shaftesbury Avenue that was decked out in lavish burlesque style for a private party.

In keeping with the formal dress code request on the invite I'd been emailed a week or two prior, I'd gone in full Scottish kilt, partly because I'm Scottish, but also as an intentional nod to my host in honor of his chosen outfit when we first met. As it turned out, I was conspicuously overdressed.

As attractive hosts and hostesses—some of them in costume, others in drag—circulated among the hundred or so guests with cocktails, I clocked Calvin Ayre and Stefan Matthews standing nearby chatting to fellow guests and enjoying the vibe. Both came over, we did the usual introductions, and at that point Ayre leaned in and whispered quietly in my ear.

"Craig will be here soon. I'll introduce you when he arrives," he told me. Ayre and Matthews moved away while my wife and I talked to each other while I simultaneously scanned the room for potential material.

Half an hour or so later, Craig Wright appeared dressed head to toe in trademark suit with a smoking jacket with large, white lapels. I didn't actually see him arrive; he just suddenly materialized in the room as if he'd slipped under the door like a vapor.

Immediately, Calvin Ayre planted a champagne cocktail in his hand, grabbed him lightly by the arm, and brought him toward me.

"This is Mark—the writer who is working on the book about Bitcoin," Ayre said.

I don't recall exactly what Wright said in response, but what I do know for sure is that he didn't actually introduce himself by name. That struck me as being a bit odd. As I studied the man up close, I couldn't get away from the fact that when I first saw him, he reminded me of an older, slightly heavier version of Simon Cowell, with a not dissimilar face and coiffed '90s hairdo.

As our wives chatted to one side, Craig Wright and I stood in each other's company, trying to make small talk. As a lifelong fan of heavy metal music, I thought I could use our common interest as a potential icebreaker.

"Great to be in the company of a fellow metal head," I said.

"I like all kinds of music," Wright replied, staring into space.

Strike one, I thought to myself

"Do you still row on the *Concept2* rowing machine, Craig?" I asked him a little later—as someone who'd also been rowing for years in a futile attempt to defeat father time and who also knew that Wright once posted YouTube videos of his rowing efforts.

"I do," was the response.

It wasn't going well.

After a while, it became obvious that, despite my best efforts, Craig Wright just didn't *do* small talk. After I'd explained in great and probably quite boring detail how difficult it had been to get across central London by cab from our hotel to arrive at the party on time, all he said was "Very good," while looking over my shoulder.

When I attempted to engage him in more serious conversation about a forthcoming defamation case he was embroiled in with YouTube personality Peter McCormack, all I got were responses that didn't quite address my questions at best or monosyllabic mutterings at worst. It wasn't that Wright was rude or unlikeable—not at all. But my summation of our first meeting was that it was all a bit strange.

On reflection, I don't quite know what I was expecting. It wasn't as if others had talked him up into being a witty, free-styling raconteur. Indeed, if anything, I'd been subtly forewarned that Wright wasn't exactly easy. Still, I'd hoped for more—more of a real person, I suppose. As much as I was aware of his reputed Asperger's and autism diagnoses, I couldn't help feeling that there was something I was missing. Of course the man was tangibly there, but at the same time it felt like he wasn't. Craig Steven Wright was like a mirage.

"Looking forward to talking more with you in the coming months," I said.

"Thanks," he replied, again not quite addressing what I'd said.

We drifted apart and never spoke again that night. As the evening progressed and the cocktails flowed, I caught periodic glimpses of Wright through the crowd. On the first occasion, he made a dramatic dance floor intervention and was seen throwing some impressive if rather dated shapes to the music. On a later occasion, he'd shed his jacket, had looped his paisley patterned tie around his forehead like a ninja warrior, and was throwing down his own version of a Morris dance on a floor that had miraculously cleared to leave him alone in the spotlight. As this bizarre performance played out with absolutely zero self-consciousness evident on Wright's part, I made eye contact with Calvin Ayre across the dance floor. He was nodding, and smiling as if to say, "That's Craig for you." I smiled back. In that moment I got it.

My wife and I ate some finger buffet food, had a couple more drinks with some nice people in the Bitcoin world, and enjoyed what was a very pleasant evening. Not long afterwards, we bade our farewells and left the party as numbers started to thin out. As I looked back from the door though, the last image I caught was Craig Wright, solo on the dance floor again, wreathed in dry ice, a small crowd gathered around him, half encouraging, half cringing. It was astonishing. The moment was frozen in time and reminded me of David Brent's epic "dance" scene from the UK version of *The Office*: highly amusing and endearing, but at the same time just a little tragic. I smiled to myself and walked out into the London night. I couldn't begin to figure Craig Wright out, but I couldn't deny quite admiring and liking the little that I knew. Satoshi or not, the man was certainly unique.

The next morning, I emailed Calvin Ayre and thanked him for his hospitality and the introduction to Craig. I made no reference to his dance floor antics. I didn't need to. We both knew what we had seen.

"Craig is infantile in some ways and they want to use that to cancel his massive brain," Ayre said. "Craig is one of the smartest fifteen-year-olds...and he'll be that way until the day he dies. It's our job to let the world know the truth about Satoshi," he added.

CHAPTER **TWO**

nChain

The day after meeting Craig Wright, I emailed him and said it had been good to meet in person and that I was looking forward to talking more. No reply came back so I just left it. A few weeks later I emailed him again and asked if we could talk on Zoom as he'd suggested when we spoke at the party.

"For what purpose?" his email response began. "I will let you know that no number of talks will do as much as an idea on paper (other than making me less happy). Meetings do not help me align in that way if I don't know what I'm talking about. So, I require details."

On one hand I wasn't at all surprised by the tone of Wright's response, having met him face to face. I could easily imagine that that person could send such a bizarre response to a simple request to talk as we'd already agreed. At the same time, I was surprised that someone who I imagined would relish the idea of telling his story, could appear to be so resistant to telling it. Regardless, I made light of things with some kind of joke and ultimately got connected with his assistant.

"She will find some time," he said.

Rather than talk on Zoom, it was agreed that Wright and I would meet in person in his nChain office in Central London. I travelled down to London the night before, stayed in a hotel in Piccadilly, and then the next morning made my way on foot up Regent Street to Oxford Circus. I was early, so I did a quick walk-by of the address: a quiet backstreet running parallel to Oxford Street with seating areas at one end where office workers sat drinking coffee and taking periodic bites out of takeaway salads and sandwiches while staring at cell phone screens. I too sat for a while, staring at my cell phone while intermittently looking through the notes and questions I'd prepared, readying myself for what I hoped would be a constructive meeting with someone who might be the creator of Bitcoin. At 1:50 p.m., I stood up and turned back to face the street behind me. nChain's office was on the corner on my left and was almost entirely glass fronted with a reception lobby with a desk on the right and an elevator straight ahead.

I walked in the main door as others filed out, entered the elevator, pushed the button for the fifth floor, and arrived in another reception area with a row of comfortable seats on one side with a large nChain sign on the wall behind it that faced a TV screen mounted on the opposite wall. It was dead silent. The TV screen was blank and I was alone. After a while I was still alone. I started to wonder if I had the correct time or indeed the right day for our meeting. After a few more minutes, a casually dressed male appeared and looked vaguely in my direction.

"Need anything?" he said.

"I'm here to see Craig Wright at two p.m.," I told him.

Without saying a word, the young man pointed to a corridor bounded by head-high glass partitions on the right and a long, glass-fronted office on the left. I walked along the corridor and from the end I could see a large area of glass cubicles with people hard at work ahead of me, evidently the gritty coalface of the work that nChain was engaged with day to day. On my left I could see Craig Wright sitting behind a desk in the long office in a suit and tie with headphones on and engaged in what looked like a video call. I knocked on the glass office door at the same time as holding a hand up to acknowledge to Wright that I had arrived. He in turn waved me in while pointing to a small leather sofa at the opposite end of the room.

As he did so, I continued taking notes and readying the spare iPhone I always used to record conversations while also noticing that Wright didn't sit still, even on video calls. Indeed, as he talked, he swung his revolving office chair from side to side, sometimes to the point that he must have been side on to his caller. After a couple of minutes, he wrapped up the call, walked over, and shook my hand before asking if I wanted a coffee. I said yes and he walked back to the door, said something to a blonde girl in the cubicle opposite his office and returned, sat down, and crossed his legs.

"So here I am again with Satoshi Nakamoto," I said, smiling.

Wright didn't answer. He looked uncomfortable and adjusted his jacket that he'd sat down on while waiting for me to replace my opening line with something that would be easier for him to digest. Instead, I gave him more of the same.

"Does it bother you when other people claim to be Satoshi Nakamoto?" I asked him this question specifically because the weekend prior I'd been sent an article about a book that was being published that claimed a former NHS employee named James Bilal Caan, who lived in a small village in Yorkshire, was Satoshi.

"Of course, because they're stupid," Wright said, suddenly looking quite weary and resigned. "I mean, let's see, Paul Le Roux for example. I helped the Feds put him in jail. He had nothing to do with Bitcoin. The only reason his name ever gets mentioned is because I was connected to having him arrested."

Unexpectedly, Wright appeared to be on a roll. He seemed much more energized by the idea of dismantling the arguments for would-be Satoshis than discussing or arguing his own case.

"Hal Finney," Wright began. "Hal had no fucking idea about how economics worked. Nice guy, great developer. But being a great developer isn't enough to do Bitcoin. James Donald. James Donald I had a fricking argument with when I was Satoshi. People thought I was giving him compliments but they were actually put-downs."

"Nick Szabo?" I suggested.

"He's a tool," Wright said.

"What about the one that was in the papers over the weekend?" I asked.

"Chaldean numbers, that's all. If you add up the letters of his name and all that crap..." Wright replied, rolling his eyes in disgust before mentally swiveling to a complete tangent. I was happy to let him go.

"What people forget is that there was a whole digital currency industry bigger than today's that crashed in the '90s," he began. "Chaum. DigiCash. He's the one everyone talks about but there were lots of them. Zookoo, the guy behind Zcash. He was another anarchist and he seems to forget his own past. A lot of people in this industry do that."

"OK, but if this stuff has been around forever, why has it never got anywhere," I asked him.

"Anarchists," Wright replied. "Chaum was an anarchist and so were a lot of these guys. He tried to make a version of money that the government couldn't interact with."

"So, from a layman's perspective, is the idea that Bitcoin is designed to be invisible to governments the biggest myth of all?" I asked, keen to get some kind of stake in the ground to anchor the story.

"Of course it is. It's a fucking blockchain. You can trace everything. What it does is stop the NSA from tracing everything. It goes back to the old-fashioned way of policing where I go to you,

you rat that guy, and then he rats another guy and we work up the chain. That's how we protect privacy because the cops have just enough to go after the big guys while leaving all the little shit alone."

"So the ideology was wrong?" I said.

"Yes. Everyone wants to say that Bitcoin was the first decentralized cryptocurrency, but for one it isn't a cryptocurrency, and two it's not the first to be decentralized," said Wright.

"Why isn't it a cryptocurrency?" I asked him.

"It's not encrypted, and neither is it a currency. It's digital cash. Cash isn't currency. Currency is a form of legal tender that must be accepted. Bank money is currency. It's not encrypted because it uses hashing algorithms but it's clear text. Every transaction can be viewed, monitored, and checked, by anyone. It's just an electronic cash system."

"And the key is that it can scale?" I added, knowing full well that I was opening up a juicy area of the debate that Wright might relish.

"I had a fight about this before I even launched Bitcoin with James Donald. I said, 'Look, Bitcoin ends up in data centers.' I told him that eventually Bitcoin would end up with block sizes equivalent to two DVDs worth—which is not small. Everyone said, 'Oh but the government will come and interact and take it over,' and I said, 'For fuck sake, this isn't anti-government.'"

It was becoming clear to me that if I gave Craig Wright the opportunity to philosophize about something he appeared to have invented, he'd happily talk all day and descend down all manner of political, mathematical, and theoretical rabbit holes in the process.

However, I couldn't ignore something that seemed important. Even I got the sense after just an hour in the man's company, that he knew just too much and was able to tackle questioning and challenges without the slightest of hesitation. As much as I wanted to doubt him and to look for chinks in his armor, there was little to doubt from a surface credibility standpoint. This wasn't a man that appeared to have to think too much about what he was saying. I wasn't seeing the cogs of his brain grinding around trying to summon a plausible answer from somewhere. I'd interviewed a lot of people in my career. I'd seen every type of body language and had heard all kinds of bullshit. But it all appeared to come far too naturally to Craig Wright. I was already considering that it was unlikely that he wasn't Satoshi Nakamoto. He seemed to know too much.

However, in our first formal meeting I wanted to know more about the person and less about the invention. And that's where things became a little more difficult. Wright would riff all day about obscure subjects like Arrow's Theorem and elliptical curves. That was clearly his comfort zone where he felt most like himself. Whenever I asked him about his *actual* self however, Wright showed a different side. Rather than want to talk, it seemed like he wanted to shut down any meaningful exploration of his personality.

One of things I wanted to explain to Wright before we talked about his life was that I wanted to tell a fair and balanced history of Bitcoin and to do that it would be ludicrous if he and aspects of his personality and life story weren't central to it. As much as there were Wright doubters, nothing had happened since 2015 to push a more convincing Satoshi candidate forward into the world.

"I think it might be helpful to humanize you a little," I began. "People have an impression of you that may not be accurate. This could be an opportunity to redress that and to show the world the real Craig Wright."

As I spoke, Wright continued to shift uncomfortably in his chair and downed his double espresso in one shot before walking to his office door and asking his assistant for another.

"You see, this is what most people don't understand," he said. "I'm not a fucking normal person. I'm not like you. I'm not like anyone who might read about Bitcoin. I really don't want to be put in a box of any kind. Some people don't just belong in a box."

"When did you first realize you suffered from Asperger's?" I asked him.

"I got told back when I was seventeen at school," he said.

"Did you struggle at school?"

"No, but I didn't do well on a social level," Wright said.

"You weren't a jock type who went out for beers then?"

"Well, sometimes I did. But even then I didn't really belong."

"How about nowadays?"

"I don't get people properly."

"You mean like me emailing you out of the blue to arrange a Zoom call?" I said, half joking.

"Yes, like that. But this is much better. I need to get to know people. Sometimes, I come across a lot harsher than I mean to. I can be a total arsehole sometimes," Wright said.

"Maybe, behind the mask, you're a good guy really?" I proposed.

Wright, a little ironically, ignored the obvious reference I'd made to alter egos hidden behind masks.

"Yes, well, sometimes I'm blunt. People take stuff I say the wrong way and it's easy to waste time on social media bullshit."

"You do a lot of social media though. In fact your communications on your blog have become increasingly blunt lately," I said.

"People like me want to shift the world to fit their worldview. Sometimes the world kicks and screams a little. It doesn't want to shift. I don't negotiate. Wait, actually I do, but not how people think."

"What do you mean?" I asked.

"If you're wanting to buy something from me I'll give you the lowest price first and work up. I'm opposite. If you start negotiating and wasting my time, I'm going to add. People out in the world should take note of this. I'll start low and it will get worse. There's a time value to my negotiations, so if you're fucking around with me, I'll add cost."

"I'll remember that the next time I'm trying to buy something from you…" I joked.

Wright didn't laugh. Whether he meant it or not, it seemed to me that he was subtly referencing the position he was currently in, whereby he was suing people for stealing his intellectual property and others for defamation.

"Do you think a day will come when crypto-exchanges offload BTC altogether?" I asked, referring to what Wright supporters saw as the illegitimate version of Bitcoin controlled by people who didn't believe Wright was Satoshi and who were corrupting his life's work.

"Hopefully they'll get rid of exchanges altogether," Wright said. "To me they're just bucket shops. They all need to go away."

"Okay, can we get back to *you*?"

"People won't understand me and what people don't get is that I don't feel the need to be understood. Why should I? I just want to work and study and be left alone."

"That's unrealistic," I said. "Surely you realize that once you were revealed to be Satoshi, life was going to change forever? People are going to want to know who you really are," I said.

"That's not my problem. And people don't always get what they want," Wright said. "That's not how life works."

I was starting see why Wright found navigating people's expectations of him, and by extension, life in general, such a frustrating business. Wright never wanted to be revealed as Satoshi and even when he was, he failed to see why he needed to conform to what people thought Satoshi Nakamoto—a legitimately mythical figure in the context of the modern internet age—should be. Rather than being something he needed to worry about, Wright saw other people's opinion of him as their problem, not his. Despite overwhelming demands for more proof and endless accusations of being a fraud since 2015, Wright seemed unwilling to waste his time discussing it, far less trying to prove anything to silence doubters.

"You'll never satisfy these people," he said. "They're just trolls."

Instead, he said, he'd work, be with his family, and would happily let lawyers sort the defamation and IP issues out in court.

"Maybe not, but would you not rather people had a chance to understand you rather than relying on what's out there and perhaps made up?" I asked.

"How I am goes all the way back to my childhood," Wright said, pivoting again.

"Well let's go there," I said. "But first, why Satoshi Nakamoto at all?"

"I was always interested in Japanese culture. That goes back to my grandfather," he said. "But it didn't need deep thought. Satoshi just means 'ash' and, honestly, it was meant to be a funny reference to Pokémon. Nakamoto is the surname of a Japanese monk who was the equivalent of Adam Smith. But simply the name was just a way to work and still have some privacy."

Although little is known about the granular detail of Craig Wright's early life, there's little doubt that he used his relationship with his abusive father, Frederick Wright, as motivation for everything he would later achieve.

Wright senior was in the military and served in Vietnam in the 8th Battalion in the Australian Army.

"He saw many of his friends die in Vietnam," Wright says. "I'm not sure that he ever recovered."

By the time Wright was born in Brisbane in October 1970, his father was drinking and was already being violent toward Wright's mother. Wright, shy, awkward, and introverted as a child, was just not his father's type of son.

"He never admired me. I was never fucking good enough. We played chess from when I was three or four and if I made a wrong move he'd wallop me. We clashed right from the beginning," Wright told author Andrew O'Hagan in 2016 for his article in *London Review of Books*.

When Wright's father left the family when Wright was just ten years old, young Craig gravitated toward his grandfather Ronald Lynam, who had also served in the Australian military having been awarded the first Marconi School of Wireless degree in Australia.

By all reports, Wright's grandfather was also a spy who was well versed in cryptography and early computer technology. It is also said that Lynam worked on trying to break the Japanese encoding system called "Purple Machine," a commercial version of Germany's Enigma machine purchased by the Japanese navy in the early 1930s.

With no father in the house as a role model, Wright found himself gravitating toward his grandfather, in whose house he would spend countless hours in the basement looking at logbooks and computer paraphernalia. Before long, he was interested in hacking and code and was even starting to experiment with writing his own to a level far above what was normal for a kid his age.

"My grandfather was an incredibly important part of my childhood," Wright says. "My mother was a single parent and worked more than one job. I spent a lot of time at his house while he looked after me, and, to keep me quiet, he'd often give me math problems to solve. At the time, I thought these were very important but really he was just keeping me out of his hair."

While Wright learned rudimentary electrical engineering and cryptography, he also became interested in Japanese culture, history, and martial arts. By the time he was a teenager, rather than playing sports like other kids of his age, Wright was dressing up in Japanese martial arts outfits carrying Samurai swords and playing Dungeons and Dragons—all to the embarrassment of his two sisters.

"I was never very comfortable with the social side of being a teenager," Wright says. "I was the kind of person that the other kids might have wanted on the football team because I played quite well, but that was the only reason they wanted me on the team. *He can play, but otherwise fuck him,* was what people probably thought."

At eighteen, Wright followed his grandfather's path and joined the air force after graduating from Padua College High School in Melbourne in 1987.

"They didn't know what to do with me," Wright says. "So I was sent to work in a bunker to do the coding for a bombing system. They needed solutions fast and I could give them those."

After leaving the air force, Wright had a major health scare where he had to have a patch of melanoma removed from his back. He had to have several skin grafts. "It was stage four," says Wright. "But after the skin grafts, it disappeared."

While learning to become a chef on the side, Wright went to the University of Queensland to study for what would be his first of many degrees, in computer systems engineering. This would begin a lifelong quest for learning that continues to this day.

"T.S. Elliot once said that you're not educated until you've studied something you thought you'd study and that you don't enjoy," Wrights says. "I have done that on many occasions. If there's something there, I'll tick it off. I used academia as a means to undermine the lecturers teaching the crap."

After getting his first degree, Wright started forging a reputation for being an eccentric but highly efficient tech specialist able to apply himself to pretty much any solution he was presented with.

Under the umbrella of his first company—DeMorgan Information Security Systems—Wright did work for a variety of blue-chip organizations in Australia such as Vodafone and the Australian Stock Exchange, the latter as security manager.

"I helped set up the first peer-to-peer system that allowed brokers to communicate across the country," says Wright.

In 1996, having met online, Wright married his first wife Lynn, several years his elder, who was working in Ottawa, Canada as a nursing manager in an intensive care department. Wright proposed after just six weeks and produced a ring, whereupon Lynn moved to Sydney, Australia to begin a new life.

"He was very mature for twenty-six," Lynn told Andrew O'Hagan for an article in *London Review of Books*. "He always has to be the best. And the hard part about that is he left bodies by the wayside. He stepped on people."

The Wrights started working together, Craig doing the tech work and Lynn providing the support, for his burgeoning information security business.

Rob Jenkins, a UK citizen who later moved to Australia, crossed paths with Wright in 1999 while working at Vodafone, the world's largest telecommunications company at that time. Jenkins' role was to create online customer service interfaces and he ran into Wright when seeking to implement better online security with firewalls.

"Craig was involved with every aspect of the build," Jenkins says. "To this day I have never seen anything so secure."

Even in 1999, Wright had the reputation of being one of the best in his field with an incredible eye for detail. As he would do with many of the people he did work for as a contractor, Wright struck up a friendship with Jenkins that has lasted to the present day.

"We created the Asia-Pac firewall and control system. At the time there were no firewalls that could handle the number of customers of Vodafone at that time—1.5 million users. Cisco couldn't create that kind of firewall system, but we did," Wright explains.

After Jenkins left Vodafone and moved into roles in the Australian banking sector, he says their conversations changed. Given Jenkins's job, he and Wright discussed banking, security, and the concept of money in general. The two men even went as far as to ruminate on whether there was scope for a digital form of money that could replace existing financial systems with an immutable ledger that could be replicated across multiple systems. They also discussed ideas that had existed in the past such as E-Gold, a system that delivered a gold-backed digital currency, minus the idea of blockchain backup.

Around the same time as the Vodafone work, Wright also did work for Lasseters, the first licensed gaming / casino company.

"I set up the security infrastructure as well as payment and logging systems. They were losing money because the US government had restricted payments through the Swift system. Because of this restriction, Lasseters weren't able to transfer money into Australia from Europe or Malaysia," Wright explains. "As a solution to that I was working on a token-based payment system that would have allowed instant settlement across banks internationally."

The picture that can be developed is that Wright, while building a reputation as a hardworking information security expert able to develop bespoke systems for a variety of companies across sectors like telecommunications, leisure, banking, and finance, was also, on the side, formulating a carefully created plan of his own that would eventually lead to Bitcoin.

The start point, however, was long before 2008.

Wright has been open about saying that Tim May's Blacknet was an inspiration for him, in the same way as Adam Back's Hashcash and Wei Dai's B-Money had been. May's Blacknet, however, was the beginning of everything for him.

Born in 1951, Timothy C. May was a technical writer, engineer, and once a senior scientist at Intel. In addition, he is generally considered to be the founder of the crypto-anarchist movement whose values centered on principles such as privacy and political and economic freedom achieved via the use of cryptographic software. May agitated in the cypherpunk community throughout the 1980s and wrote *The Crypto-Anarchist Manifesto* in 1988. In 1993, May dispensed with the theorizing and put his ideas into practice with Blacknet, the aim of which was described succinctly in a description that read:

> *"Blacknet is nominally nondideological [sic], but considers nation-states, export laws, patent laws, national security considerations and the like to be relics of the pre-cyberspace era. Export and patent laws are often used to explicitly project national power and imperialist, colonialist state fascism. Blacknet believes it is solely the responsibility of a secret holder to keep that secret—not the responsibility of the State, or of us, or of anyone else who may come into possession of that secret. If a secret's worth having, it's worth protecting."*

Initially released anonymously, Blacknet operated as what amounted to as an early forerunner of Wikileaks, where third parties were invited to give information anonymously in return for crypto-credits, a closed loop form of currency. Wright liked the idea of Blacknet and wanted to take the concepts further in conjunction with the best elements of Adam Back's Hashcash, a proof of work algorithm where computers performed small tasks that could be instantly verified, and Wei Dai's B-Money, which described the concept of an untraceable network where senders and receivers used pseudonyms to identify themselves. These pseudonyms were really "public keys" or addresses, which, when matched to private keys, would provide access to the addresses.

"I admired B-Money," Wright told Andrew O'Hagan. "And it definitely gave me some of the cryptographic code that ended up in the first version of Bitcoin."

In early 2004, Wright started working on his own project, confusingly titled Blacknet (note minor spelling difference).

"Blacknet was a secure economically enabled version of the internet," says Wright. "I was trying to develop ideas around micro-payments, cents, or even fractions of a cent, in exchange for, for example, single pages of information. And I did this because credit card payments for the same would have been far too expensive."

It was while working on Blacknet that Wright had one of several eureka moments.

"By accident I discovered what later became a solution to Bitcoin," says Wright. "Blacknet didn't go anywhere but not because it didn't work. It *did* work, but it did so by relying on anonymity and I realized that an anonymous system could never be scaled to the world. Indeed, the only people that an anonymous system would benefit were criminals wishing to conduct black-market trade. I had no interest in creating money for that purpose."

Wright joined the audit firm BDO in November 2004 because he needed hands-on auditing experience. "I'd studied accountancy, but there's a huge difference between studying in a classroom and doing the job in the real world. So I went to BDO to learn how these systems work at a deep level."

Wright pulled every element of his background and training into his planning for creating Bitcoin, cherry-picking his academic studies and his practical work with the specific intention of accruing all the elements required for such an ambitious idea as a new form of digital cash that could potentially revolutionize the world.

"The first time he mentioned this concept he called it digital money. We were just chatting about computer programs (I think) and he said he felt the way of the future was digital money," Wright's ex-wife Lynn recalls.

At BDO, Wright was engaged by, among other entities, the South Australian Police where Wright did a forensic analysis of digital networks to track down child grooming perpetrators. According to Wright, a pedophile ring was apparently brought down as a result of his work.

It was while he was working at BDO that Wright met Stefan Matthews who was working with the sports betting company Centrebet in 2005 in his capacity as Chief Information Officer.

"We were in the process of preparing for an IPO and it was my job to source an audit firm to oversee the process," Matthews recalls. "And the successful firm was BDO."

"Craig was responsible for overseeing the audit group that looked at all of our control systems to ensure that they were complaint and not open to online vulnerabilities. We were dealing with customer funds so there was a lot of security expertise required. Craig Wright had an enormous number of credentials in this area. His technical understanding was second to none," Matthews explains.

As much as Matthews identified Wright's ability to do the job he was tasked to do, Matthews also saw a couple of different sides to Wright in these early interactions.

"Craig seemed to really care about solving clients' specific problems," Matthews recalls. "As far as his personal skills were concerned, he was undoubtedly a little different. Craig was a bit eccentric."

Wright continued as the primary point of contact between Centrebet and BDO for several years thereafter. In parallel, Wright and Matthews continued to have separate conversations about topics outside of his responsibilities to Centrebet.

"Craig started talking to me about a whole raft of subjects and concepts related to electronic cash and digital currencies. This was interesting to me because we worked in an industry where the processing of payments to and from customers was critical. Craig spoke a lot about immutable ledgers, and he was discussing them in the context of tracking security events on our network. This would have been sometime in 2007," Matthews explains.

These conversations entirely fit in with the Bitcoin trajectory. By 2007, Wright was already pulling together all the economic, financial, and coding elements required to assemble his vision for digital cash—and all of it was underpinned by the singular concept of an immutable ledger where every transaction on the blockchain could be observed and traced. The planning for Satoshi Nakamoto's revolutionary white paper was already underway.

"Before I wrote the final version of the paper, I wrote the code. And I did this to make sure that, before I committed fully, it would work," Wright explains.

Wright set up what's called an MVP, a Minimum Viable Product, essentially a prototype of Bitcoin to test whether the code would work in a domestic setting.

"Once I knew it could work and scale, I knew it was worth taking the idea further," Wright says.

Emboldened by the initial success of his MVP, Wright started documenting, in a combination of handwritten notes and Dragon voice-type software, the first version of what would become the Bitcoin white paper.

"I started writing in August of 2007," Wright says. "I'd write some, leave it, and come back. It took until March of 2008 to get the full eighty pages."

Wright, still an employee of BDO, had wanted to develop his digital cash idea within BDO and pitched the idea to his boss at the time, Allan Granger, with whom he had a meeting in August of 2007.

"I was hoping to use the data centers within BDO because otherwise it was going to be expensive. To use the data center, I needed Allan Granger's sign off."

Apparently, this request was rejected, albeit that Granger arranged meetings for Wright with other BDO employees while Wright negotiated a clause in his contract that allowed him to work on his own projects such as Bitcoin in his own time.

"I took a lower salary to facilitate doing my own projects," Wright says.

Wright sent the initial draft out to trusted confidants for feedback sometime in 2008. One such recipient was his uncle Donald Lynam, who Wright had always viewed as one of his role models.

Donald Lynam had been a Wing Commander in the Australian Air Force for thirty years before leaving and joining the Department of Defence in Canberra to work in the areas of information technology and logistics management. Lynam would become a member of The Order of Australia, one of the country's highest recognitions for individuals who did "conspicuous good deeds" for the community in which they operated.

"I received the advanced and pretty rough copy of the white paper in probably mid-2008," Lynam says. "Craig sent me a copy for my review but it was too technical and poorly written. Although it wasn't actually called Bitcoin at that time, it was clearly to be a digital monetary system."

"Don received what would have been the alpha version of the white paper and basically ripped it apart. I can remember not being very happy about that," Wright laughs.

A white paper is meant to sell a concept clearly. Wright's iteration as it stood did not. Whoever he showed it to seemed to struggle with the complexities to the extent that the concept wasn't as persuasive as Wright needed it to be.

"I have a vague memory of the white paper. I think I proofread a part of it, but to be honest, whenever I read it for the content my eyes just glazed over," Lynn Wright remembers.

Frustrated, Wright contacted his American friend Dave Kleiman on March 12th, 2008, with a request. In an email, he wrote:

> *"I need your help editing a paper I am going to release later this year. I have been working on a new form of electronic money. Bit cash, Bitcoin...*
>
> *You are always there for me Dave. I want you to be part of it all.*
>
> *I cannot release it as me. GMX, Vistomail and Tor. I need your help and I need a version of me to make this work that is better than me."*—Craig

As much as Wright and Dave Kleiman had become friends after running into each other in cryptography forums as far back as 2003, from all reports they were fundamentally different types of people but who shared several common interests. Where Wright was introverted and socially awkward, Kleiman, a burly army veteran from Florida, was an alpha-male type who loved big trucks, contact sports, and hard living. Yet, somehow, these two men, separated by thousands of miles, became fast friends online.

Kleiman mostly sat at a computer, following a motorcycle accident in 1995 when he was just twenty-eight that confined him permanently to a wheelchair. Having been an active, good-time guy who enjoyed the outdoors, Kleiman was forced to focus his attentions elsewhere. And that elsewhere reputedly encompassed drugs, online gambling, and his own computer company called Computer Forensics LLC.

"I knew Craig trusted Dave as a good friend and a fellow information security specialist. I also knew Craig and Dave would discuss projects and articles they were writing," Lynn Wright remembers. "When I first met Dave, Craig and I were in Florida for a conference. To finally meet Dave was wonderful and they were genuinely happy to see each other. They responded to each other like brothers, first joking and teasing each other, then getting into technical conversations at which my eyes again glazed over."

It is assumed that Kleiman, seemingly a more gifted writer than Wright, fulfilled his friend's request by polishing up the white paper into something more consistent with the version that exists today. He had been cryptically pre-warned that his help would be required in an email from Wright at the end of December 2007 that read: "Nothing now, but I want your help with something big soon."

And Kleiman, as always, was there for his Australian friend.

As such, before long, the paper had gone from an eighty-page diatribe of the workings of Craig Wright's mind vomited onto the page, to a streamlined document ready to change the world. To the best of anyone's knowledge, Kleiman's edit was his only involvement with the Bitcoin white paper and, by extension, the creation of Bitcoin. But it was a vital step. By June 2008, after some back and forth with Kleiman, Wright had a solid idea to go into battle with. The following month, he walked into Stefan Matthews's office at Centrebet and handed him a USB stick.

"This was one of the many occasions where Craig came in wanting to discuss projects. I didn't always have the time; I had so much to do of my own. But he had so much passion. He always wanted to involve me in whatever he was doing," Matthews says.

On the USB stick was something much more fully-formed than the notional ideas and concepts Wright had been riffing about for the previous year while his friend mostly tuned him out. This was something far more definitive and tangible. He was showing Matthews the famous Bitcoin white paper.

Wright told Matthews he should read the document that was on the USB. Matthews wasn't a fan of reading documents on screens, so he put the USB into his computer, copied the contents, and then printed a hard copy for himself. The document Matthews read did not contain the words Satoshi Nakamoto, but was titled "Bitcoin."

"I skim-read the whole thing," Matthews remembers. "I definitely read the abstract and browsed the various headings. I immediately recognized what I was reading as basically a consolidation of some of the concepts Craig had been talking to me about for months. To that extent there was no great reaction."

Wright was testing the water in advance of launching his product, and to do that he had to take the idea to the people who would understand it. One such person was Wei Dai, the Chinese computer engineer famous for creating the distributed electronic cash system B-Money that Wright had been so enamored with.

On August 22nd, 2008, Wright, as his alter ego Satoshi Nakamoto, emailed Wei Dai to break some important news. Satoshi referenced communication he'd had earlier with Hashcash creator Adam Back—communication Back has vowed to never release to the public.

"I was very interested to read your b-money page. I'm getting ready to release a paper that expands on your ideas into a complete working system. Adam Back (hashcash.org) noticed the similarities and pointed me to your site. I need to find out the year of publication of your B-Money page for the citation in my paper," Satoshi wrote while also attaching a pre-release draft for Dai's perusal.

"Thanks for letting me know about your paper. I will take a look at it and will let you know if I have any comments or questions," Dai replied.

CHAPTER **THREE**

Genesis

*"**I**'ve been working on a new electronic cash system that's fully peer-to-peer, with no trusted third party."*

The email to the cryptography mailing list at metzowd.com landed with a thud at 6:10 p.m. UTC on October 31st, 2008. The subject line simply read, "Bitcoin P2P e-cash paper," and the communication was signed, simply, Satoshi Nakamoto, a pseudonym contactable at the email address satoshin@gmx.com.

Within the content of the message there was a link alerting readers to a white paper entitled *Bitcoin: A Peer-to-Peer Electronic Cash System* which was available to read in PDF format at a website called bitcoin.org, the domain for which had been registered several weeks prior.

A white paper is an information document published by an individual or company to introduce or highlight a product, solution, or service that it plans to offer. In the cryptography world they are commonplace. In Satoshi Nakamoto's case, the Bitcoin white paper (the word Bitcoin appears in it just twice) was presenting a revolutionary decentralized (not reliant on a central authority) system of online cash that required no trusted third party intermediary—a bank for example—and where one of the primary USPs of Satoshi's vision was that the issue referred to as "double-spending"—where someone could theoretically spend the same electronic "coin" twice—had been solved by virtue of fixed protocols that ensured that each coin was unique and therefore couldn't be destroyed or replicated.

For years, a double-spending solution had been a brick wall for would-be creators of digital cash. Ever since the early 1990s, several revered experts on the subject had attempted to address the main conundrum that acted as a barrier to the progress of early attempts to create electronic cash systems. In some cases the interplay between traceability and privacy had been the key issue. With increased traceability, privacy decreased.

Some proposed the assignation of an independent "observer" to the network to, in effect, "police" double-spending perpetrators. In essence, this amounted to the creation of a trusted third party or central authority, an idea that defeated the point somewhat. This idea also came with privacy issues of its own in addition to increased transaction costs, which in turn would make micro-payments prohibitively expensive.

But now, in 2008, there *was* a workable method and it's important to stress that Satoshi's solution drew inspiration from the best features of many previous attempts to solve the problem. Chinese engineer Wei Dai's "B-Money" from 1998 was one. British cryptographer Adam Back's "Hashcash" from 2002, was another. With Bitcoin, Satoshi appeared to have cracked the secret to a system that ensured a kind of digital scarcity that nobody previously had.

As such, the possibilities for commerce highlighted by Satoshi's idea were truly world-bending if they worked. And the cryptography world, a community that had been fascinated by the idea of anonymity, privacy, and by extension, alternate cash systems since the cypherpunk days of the 1980s, took notice, albeit with a significant degree of caution.

Where Satoshi's vision diverged from two of the key tenets of cypherpunk ideology—privacy through anonymity and censorship resistance—was that Bitcoin as a concept was not fixated with anonymity at all. Indeed, Satoshi has since stated that anonymity would have only benefitted corrupt governments and criminals. Instead, Bitcoin was geared toward the concept of privacy via *pseudonymity* in the sense that, with Bitcoin, the address at which a person received digital coins was their pseudonym and was public.

This concept of privacy through pseudonymity was the very basis on which Bitcoin, and for that matter its inventor Satoshi Nakamoto, existed.

Instead of being an anarchic idea founded on a mistrust of central banks and authority generally, Satoshi proposed Bitcoin not as a means to overthrow banks, but simply as a way by which one person anywhere could transact directly with another person anywhere else cheaply, using digital coins. All of this was designed in a manner that was transparent, promoted the rule of the law and discouraged shadowy corruption and criminality.

In the background, fixed protocols, not middlemen, served to "govern" the system. These protocols in turn were underpinned by an immutable "ledger" on the blockchain—a "plumbing" system of sorts designed to maintain a permanent record of transactions that are visible in real time to all computers linked across a network and maintained by incentivized Bitcoin "miners" around the world. This ledger of Bitcoin transactions would grow over time and would be "forever," and visible to anyone forever.

Miners were and are a key part of the Bitcoin blueprint. In simple terms, the miner's role in Bitcoin is to process transactions via a consensus algorithm entitled Proof of Work (POW), where miners compete against each other to solve complex mathematical "puzzles" so that transactions can be verified for each "block" on the blockchain / permanent ledger. To achieve this task, a powerful computer is required. Once a miner solves the puzzle for a particular block, that block is then broadcast to the network to be quickly verified by other miners. Once approved, that block is added to the ledger. From there, the process continues. Meanwhile, the successful miner receives what's called a block reward (currently 6.25 bitcoins) for winning what amounts to a giant lottery among miners, along with a fluctuating transaction fee that is in effect shaved off the Bitcoin created.

It is these miners' job therefore to mine every bitcoin, and Satoshi's white paper stated from day one that there would only ever be 21 million bitcoin created—approximately 19 million of which had already been mined by January 2023. The Bitcoin protocol has a function coded in that reduces the number of new coins issued with each new block. This is a process called "halving" and it occurs every four years.

To that extent, Bitcoin provided a degree of certainty unlike, say, the Federal Reserve in the sense that it is the Bitcoin code and not an arbitrary group of people that decides how it is issued. Some saw that as positive. However, because of Bitcoin's transparency and controlled method of supply, others have inevitably latched onto Bitcoin as being not just digital cash to be used and to spend for goods or services, but as a store of value akin to gold.

Consequently, in the years since Bitcoin's birth, many people have not used Bitcoin in the manner that Satoshi intended it to be used. Instead, many early adopters have "held" bitcoin—some from day one at a time when it had no value at all—in the hope that scarcity would cause its value to increase, which it did.

In late 2008 and early 2009, however, value in Bitcoin was a distant concept. Wright was more focused on getting his invention up and running without hardware failure. Having published the white paper in October and had assorted email communications for a month as Satoshi with James Donald, John Levine, and Ray

Dillinger, all of whom found a degree of fault, and Half Finney, who was much more positive and hopeful, Wright again wrote to his friend Dave Kleiman on December 27:

"My wife will not be happy. I am not going back to work. I need time to get my idea going…the presentation was good and the paper is out. I am already getting shit from people and attacks on what we did. The bloody bastards are wrong and I friken showed it, they should stick to the science and piss off with their politicized crap. I need your help. You edited my paper and now I need you to aid me build my idea."

Wright took the next step into the unknown on January 3, 2009 when creating what's known as the Genesis block, the hard-coded block that would serve to anchor Bitcoin on the blockchain for eternity.

The Genesis block—block 0—was unique, however, and not just because it wasn't mined. Embedded in it, and eternally inscribed on the blockchain, were the words: "The Times 03/Jan/2009 Chancellor on brink of second bailout for banks," which was a headline from that day's *Times* newspaper published in the UK.

Inevitably, people overanalyzed the text for months and still to this day. Some saw it as merely a date stamp to commemorate a momentous day; others saw it as some kind of cryptic reference related to how Bitcoin was intended to be the antidote for the inherent instability of banking institutions at a time when the world was still reeling from the financial crisis of 2008.

"It was simple," Wright says. "The threat to nationalize the banks just pissed me off. Chancellor Darling was threatening to nationalize the banks. But beyond that it was an anchor that all software synchronized open to show that nothing could have happened "live" on Bitcoin before January 3rd, 2009. I wanted to illustrate the blockchain's transparency. I signaling that that were no secrets."

Unlike all other bitcoin that would be mined after January 3rd, 2009, the genesis block bitcoin can never be spent.

"Few people understood how difficult the beginning of Bitcoin actually was," Wright says. "I needed a series of machines to run and send and receive information and to do so without fail."

In his ranch in Bagnoo, a tiny rural town located two hundred and fifty miles from Sydney with roughly fifty residents, Wright had a battery of hardware set up that he hoped would provide early Bitcoin with the stability it so desperately needed. Wright had to drive almost four hours from his home to reach this rural outpost.

"I had racks of computers in an outbuilding I'd converted. I paid to have fiber optic internet laid to the town give me the speed Bitcoin needed and everyone in the surrounding area benefitted from it," Wright explains.

Despite his thorough preparation, the first mined version of Bitcoin after the genesis block—block 1—crashed for technical reasons that were related to the types of Windows Server licenses he was using. Wright's servers crashed and had to be hurriedly reconfigured.

"The network forked and split, it was a big mess to say the least," Wright wrote in his www.craigwright.net blog.

After a frantic trip to Bagnoo from the city to reconfigure the system, Wright restored his network and Bitcoin has been running ever since. In addition to Wright, a few others were running machines as well. Dave Kleiman was running one full-time and a couple intermittently. Hal Finney, a renowned computer scientist in California was running one, and a few others were also. In total, it is estimated seventy-five machines worldwide were running Bitcoin at the beginning of 2009.

Meanwhile, Wright was still juggling his Bitcoin endeavors with the end of his tenure at BDO while trying to explain to Lynn why he wasn't going to look for another job (albeit he did briefly consider taking a position at Microsoft in Seattle, a position that was ultimately kyboshed by the aftereffects of 2008 financial crisis).

"I basically came home one day and told her that I was leaving my job and wasn't going to get another," Wright says. "Let's just say that she wasn't especially happy about that."

Lynn was largely in the dark about what her husband was doing, and she wasn't the only one.

"My staff had no idea what I was doing, and I certainly wouldn't discuss what I was doing much with family either," Wright says.

It wasn't that Wright was secretive, according to Lynn, but more that he didn't feel the need to explain complicated things to her, and equally, she didn't ever feel the need to push it.

"The hardware was in the house at Lisarow and the house at our hobby farm. I did not know what each machine was for," Lynn explains. "Whenever I asked Craig what he was doing when using the machines, he would just say 'working' and I assumed it was for clients as we did 24/7 monitoring of their systems security. My concern was that my salary was not enough to meet our monthly costs but once I told him this he just swept that worry aside so there was no use arguing with him as he could become very angry and I was tired of dealing with him when he was angry."

On January 8th, 2009, the day before block 1 of Bitcoin was created, Wright emailed Hal Finney:

> *"Thought you'd like to know, the Bitcoin v0.1 release with EXE and full source code is up on Source-forgehttp://downloads.sourceforge.net/bitcoin/bit-coin-0.1.0.rar www.bitcoin.org has release notes and screenshots." Satoshi*

On the same day, a message was posted to the cryptography mailing list entitled "Bitcoin v0.1 Released" with an accompanying explanation that describes how nodes (computers running the Bitcoin software) could be set up to send and receive:

Announcing the first release of Bitcoin, a new electronic cash system that uses a peer-to-peer network to prevent double-spending. It's completely decentralized with no server or central authority. If you can keep a node running that accepts incoming connections, you'll really be helping the network a lot. Port 8333 on your firewall needs to be open to receive incoming connections.

The software is still alpha and experimental. There's no guarantee that the system's state won't have to be restarted at some point if it becomes necessary, although I've done everything I can to build in extensibility and versioning.

You can get coins by getting someone to send you some, or turn on Options->Generate Coins to run a node and generate blocks. I made the proof-of-work difficulty ridiculously easy to start with, so for a little while in the beginning a typical PC will be able to generate coins in just a few hours. It'll get a lot harder when competition makes the automatic adjustment drive up the difficulty. Generated coins must wait 120 blocks to mature before they can be spent.

There are two ways to send money. If the recipient is online, you can enter their IP address and it will connect, get a new public key and send the transaction with comments. If the recipient is not online, it is possible to send to their Bitcoin address, which is a hash of their public key that they give you. They'll receive the transaction the next time they connect and get the block it's in.

This method has the disadvantage that no comment information is sent, and a bit of privacy may be lost if the address is used multiple times, but it is a useful alternative if both users can't be online at the same time or the recipient can't receive incoming connections.

Total circulation will be 21,000,000 coins. It'll be distributed to network nodes when they make blocks, with the amount cut in half every 4 years.

first 4 years: 10,500,000 coins

next 4 years: 5,250,000 coins

next 4 years: 2,625,000 coins

next 4 years: 1,312,500 coins

etc.

When that runs out, the system can support transaction fees if needed. It's based on open market competition, and there will probably always be nodes willing to process transactions for free.

-Satoshi Nakamoto

The recipients responded positively.

On January 11th, Hal Finney, who'd been engaging with Satoshi directly for three days, posted on Twitter a tweet for the ages when he wrote, simply, *"running bitcoin."*

The following day, as if Finney's tweet wasn't momentous enough, the first ever Bitcoin transaction took place when Craig Wright as Satoshi Nakamoto sent Hal Finney ten bitcoin. Unknown to both of them, this transaction signaled the beginning of a financial and data revolution that continues to this day. Satoshi also sent bitcoin to himself, Dave Kleiman, and one other whom he won't name.

On his blog, Finney wrote his own recollections of that first, historic transaction:

> *"When Satoshi announced the first release of the software, I grabbed it right away. I think I was the first person besides Satoshi to run bitcoin. I mined block 70-something, and I was the recipient of the first bitcoin transaction, when Satoshi sent ten coins to me as a test. I carried on an email conversation with Satoshi over the next few days, mostly me reporting bugs and him fixing them.*
>
> *Today, Satoshi's true identity has become a mystery. But at the time, I thought I was dealing with a young man of Japanese ancestry who was very smart and sincere. I've had the good fortune to know many brilliant people over the course of my life, so I recognize the signs.*
>
> *After a few days, Bitcoin was running pretty stably, so I left it running. Those were the days when difficulty was 1, and you could find blocks with a CPU, not even a GPU. I mined several blocks over the next days. But I turned it off because it made my computer run hot, and the fan noise bothered me. In retrospect, I wish I had kept it up longer, but on the*

other hand I was extraordinarily lucky to be there at the beginning. It's one of those glass half full half empty things.

The next I heard of Bitcoin was late 2010, when I was surprised to find that it was not only still going, bitcoins actually had monetary value. I dusted off my old wallet, and was relieved to discover that my bitcoins were still there. As the price climbed up to real money, I transferred the coins into an offline wallet, where hopefully they'll be worth something to my heirs."

CHAPTER **FOUR**

Exit

After Bitcoin's launch in 2009, Wright continued mining and communicating as Satoshi with a community who were keen to get the best from the embryonic system of digital cash. Most of the communications could be described as teething issues and responses to queries Wright was offering to the relatively few people who were running Bitcoin. Throughout the bulk of 2009, bitcoin had almost zero value.

"I had no expectations about bitcoin ever being worth anything, far less that it hit $1000 dollars in my lifetime," Wright says. "It was all about micro-payments, so my focus was on generating volume."

Although Craig Wright had left BDO, he remained in contact with Stefan Matthews who was still working for Centrebet. From time to time, Wright would call in on his friend, usually unannounced, to update him about whatever he was doing.

"In March or April, Craig walked into my office," Matthews recalls. "As usual, he didn't care whether I was in a meeting or a phone call; he'd just walk in and sit down. Sometimes I'd have to say to him, 'Craig, do you mind?' And it was never a problem. He was thick-skinned."

The couple of months since Bitcoin's launch had been frenetic for Wright. He'd been keeping machines running up at his farm, solving technical issues as they arose, and responding to various queries and suggestions from his small army of devotees—making no money from Bitcoin to speak of.

"Craig walked in one day, sat down, and said, 'Mate, do you have five hundred dollars?'," Matthews remembers. "I thought he must have been short of money so I said, 'Happy to give you a loan, what is it you need?'"

"I don't need money," Wright said. "Do you remember Bitcoin? It just launched in January."

Matthews scanned his brain for a second, thinking of all the many conversations he and Wright had had over the previous four years.

Eventually, while Wright sat awaiting a response, Stefan Matthews's brain dredged up a lightly buried memory of the USB stick that Wright had given him the previous year—the same USB stick that he'd jammed into his desktop, printed the contents, scanned the headings before adding the thin document to the ever-growing pile on his desk, and thinking little more about it.

"Yes, I remember Bitcoin," Matthews told Wright. "But I'm not interested."

Wright wanted to give his friend 50,000 bitcoin in exchange for $500 cash—a value of one cent each.

"It just didn't excite me," Matthews recalls of the offer. "And I was pretty sure I wouldn't be able to keep track of them anyway. I just said no."

Although he couldn't have known it at the time, Stefan Matthews had just turned down 50,000 bitcoin from the first few blocks that were mined in the initial months of January 2009. These blocks were known as Satoshi blocks, and they were called this because they were mined by Satoshi himself, Craig Wright, at his farm north of Sydney.

"I honestly never thought about it again," Matthews laughs. "I'd heard so many ideas from Craig. I'd forgotten many of them. But the Bitcoin idea just wasn't for me. I thought it was the biggest load of shit going and that it would never amount to anything of value."

It would be some time before bitcoin would be of any value. Indeed, it would be October of 2009 before bitcoin was exchanged for another currency when Martti Malmi, a Finnish developer who'd offered Wright input into the development of Bitcoin exchanged 5,050 bitcoins for $5.02.

By 2010 Craig Wright was having trouble at home; his marriage to Lynn was breaking down and he moved out of the family home as the couple underwent an initial period of separation.

Simultaneously, Wright was having increasing issues with the Australian Tax Office (ATO) with whom he'd had a brief run-in a few years previously over a Research & Development expense claims he'd made for some study courses he'd been doing that they queried.

"Back when I was still at BDO, they objected to the fact that I had seven degrees and couldn't accept that my studies were related to my work even though BDO put in a letter stating the contrary," Wright says. "They thought I was studying too much and taking from other people. It ended up in the Administrative Appeals Tribunal. I challenged it and won, and the legal fees alone cost me 8K, which was more than the 6K I was claiming for."

In 2010, the issue wasn't claims for studies, the issue was Bitcoin, which in the wider world was becoming more famous on the back of the world's first "formal" Bitcoin transaction when crypto enthusiast Lazlo Hanyecz used 10,000 bitcoins to buy two large pizzas from another person named Jeremy "Jercos" Sturdivant.

Already on the tax office's radar and having rubbed them up the wrong way by winning at a tribunal, despite Bitcoin's profile steadily being elevated in the wider consciousness, Craig Wright still wasn't exactly the most popular man with the ATO, especially now that Bitcoin, a concept the ATO had little understanding of, was in the equation.

"They disliked everything about me," Wright says. "They disliked that I was claiming for R&D for Bitcoin activities from day one."

To unpick Craig Wright's issues with the Australian Tax Office would require an understanding not only of how the tax system worked at the time as far as it related to Bitcoin, but also a clear understanding of what is ultimately a rat's nest of companies that Wright was operating in Australia from 2009 onwards after he began mining bitcoin in conjunction with continuing to do security and forensic work.

The former can be summarized conceptually simply by saying that because Bitcoin was such a new concept, the ATO couldn't decide what it was in terms of income or assets, far less how tax should be applied to it. As far as Wright's companies were concerned, he had a history of being disorganized, with entity upon entity buried within other entities, all of which makes understanding exactly what did what and when, nothing more than a frustrating fool's errand.

"I came on-board in late 2010 because Craig's companies were in a state of operational disarray and he needed serious help," John Chesher says.

Chesher, a Canadian by birth who'd later moved to Australia, met Wright through a friend of his, John Keeble, a visionary mind in the chemical electronics business.

"Craig had some issues with his tax returns and his dealings with the tax office. He was a very smart boy but he was also very scattered," Chesher says. "He'd tear into a subject, get books shipped in by the carton load, and before you know it, he'd have a degree in it. Then he'd be on to the next thing. But in his slipstream he'd leave a load of chaos. It was my job to put some order not just into his businesses, but also his life."

Chesher's impression was that Craig Wright had little grasp of what required to be done from a commercial perspective to sort through and record important details of all of his various business entities.

"He had some very good ideas in forensic computing and was helping entities defend themselves. He was trying to commercialize these ideas while at the same time he was being continually harassed by the tax office. To them he was a serial audit by this stage and the fact that he'd been lodging his own tax returns—a big no-no—didn't help. He just kept putting stuff through and whenever he encountered the tax guys he'd manage to insult them somehow."

By the time John Chesher came on-board to work for Craig Wright full-time, his alter ego Satoshi Nakamoto had stepped away from communicating about Bitcoin altogether. Barring a couple of brief interjections in 2011, Satoshi Nakamoto has never been heard from again. As far as the Bitcoin world was concerned, its inventor was gone. Although Wright himself would continue to mine bitcoin and develop ideas that could be layered on top of the system that would help to scale it, Satoshi himself no longer existed publicly. It was left to the community to dictate the invention's destiny in his absence.

"People fail to understand that I stepped away from direct involvement with communicating about Bitcoin as Satoshi because I had other things happening in my life that needed my attention more," Wright says. "Bitcoin was out, it was working and users were coming around to the idea. But it didn't need Satoshi and my other business interests needed *me*. Also, people forget that I was going through a stressful divorce. As much as Satoshi was a myth, I was also a person."

Having gone quiet in late 2010, to distract himself from the problems in his personal life, Wright took what would be his last security-related job, in Venezuela of all places, in early 2011.

"I travelled to South America as part of something called a 'Jawbreaker' team. The work I was doing there was focused on disrupting child-trafficking rings. I did not bring people to justice. I worked with teams to stop things…forever," Wright says.

Wright's work for government agencies is one of the least well-known aspects of his life and it seems that the world will never fully know what he has done in that regard. What is clear is that sex-trafficking, smuggling, and underground criminal activities are concepts that Wright has continually railed against with unusual passion. Indeed, it could be suggested that creating Bitcoin was done specifically to combat the dark shadows of the world he found so distasteful.

"I designed Bitcoin to stop the need for people like me—people who worked with SAD operatives and even those acting in the tracing of funds," Wright wrote in a book entitled *Satoshi's Vision: The Art of Bitcoin* in 2019.

"I have witnessed children as young as ten with AK-47s and women who have been forced to watch the death of their children knowing that other members of the family are being held, and if they try to escape, will be killed. All of it exists because of a system that allows records to be lost," he also wrote.

The irony is that when Wright returned from Venezuela, his Bitcoin invention was being used for precisely the purpose he hoped it wouldn't: the dark web.

The dark web site Silk Road, named after the historical network of Eurasian trade routes, launched in February 2011 and operated as a hidden service on the Tor network allowing users to buy and sell goods and services anonymously using bitcoin as the currency.

"I discovered the creation I had given birth to—something I designed to bring light—was being used for all the worst reasons. Not only drugs, but also people. Silk Road didn't blatantly advertise people the way they did drugs and guns, there are other names for everything, yet people know what is being exchanged," Wright further wrote.

What made things even worse was that users were already seeing Bitcoin as a store of value rather than the micro-payments system Wright had intended it to be. He became disillusioned and started viewing Bitcoin not as a revolutionary, world-changing invention, but as a complete failure for which he was responsible.

"After two years of earning very little but spending a lot on my research, I saw what I created as it started to become the thing I despised," Wright says.

Between 2011 and 2013, Wright's business affairs only became more complicated. Companies came and went, as did close friends and loved ones. It was a period of deep transition. By 2012, Wright was formally divorced from Lynn. Meanwhile, Dave Kleiman passed away in April of 2013 from natural causes related to an MRSA infection. It is rumored that CIA agents were present at his funeral. Nobody knows why, although it certainly fueled rumors that the connections between Bitcoin and the security state ran deeper than we'll ever know.

As much as Dave Kleiman the person was gone, the complex, unfathomable trail of his business relationship with Craig Wright remain to this day. Two years before he died, perhaps to put the proceeds of his and Kleiman's Bitcoin mining efforts out of reach of the ATO, Wright apparently created an offshore trust entitled the Tulip Trust, the function of which was to hold over a million bitcoins in Kleiman's name until a future date (January 2020), whereupon the coins would revert to Wright. While it is not confirmed whether Kleiman ever actually controlled the one million plus bitcoins, in a separate agreement it was decided that Kleiman would also receive 350,000 bitcoins and it is known that those were received and stored by Kleiman on a personal hard drive.

"Craig and Dave had set up a company called W & K Info Defense LLC," Chesher says. "My understanding was that the purpose of that company was to mine bitcoins."

For whatever reason, the Tulip Trust agreement had Kleiman on edge. It is said that some of the work he and Wright had done sailed close to the edge of legality. At one point, because bitcoin had little value, it was said that they got themselves involved in illegal gambling activities in Costa Rica to raise quick capital, although none of that has been confirmed.

"Neither of us had money, physical money, we had money in Liberty, an exchange in Costa Rica..." Wright once told author Andrew O'Hagan.

In an email dated June 24th, 2011, Kleiman had expressed his concerns to Wright: "I think you are mad, and this is risky. But I believe in what we are trying to do."

Whatever Wright's reasons for creating the trust were, it seems likely that it was set up for tax reasons. After Kleiman's death, Wright was philosophical about their relationship.

"We never really thought that 'we made Satoshi.' It was good; it was done. But I don't think we realized how big it would be," he also told O'Hagan. "I loved Dave. I would have seen him more. I would have talked to him more," he added.

With Dave Kleiman gone and with BTC hitting its highest price since launch at almost $950 each, by the end of 2013, under the umbrella of one of his company's called Hotwire Preemptive Intelligence Group, Wright had real aspirations to turn Bitcoin into what would essentially be an 'official' currency in Australia.

His plan was to create a Bitcoin bank—Denariuz Bank, he wanted to call it—and to progress the idea, he and his accountant, John Chesher, sat in a number of meetings with Michael Hardy, one of the senior commissioners at the Australian Tax Office, to discuss the idea.

"It was only around this time, when Craig got me to go through all this stuff that I realized he was Satoshi Nakamoto," Chesher recalls. "Craig was saying, 'I'm going to make Bitcoin a Fiat currency. We're going to talk to the tax office and we're going to get this done in Australia.' I told him it was simply not going to happen in Australia. I told him we'd probably have lovely conversations with the tax office, but ultimately, it would go nowhere. I also told him that when it did go nowhere, it would probably come back to bite him. He was adamant though."

Nevertheless, despite his accountant's stark warnings, Wright pressed on in his quest to found the world's first Bitcoin bank. Wright and his team engaged in discussion with Michael Hardy at the tax office and by all accounts these conversations were amicable, bordering on positive. At one point, when Bitcoin's price topped a certain level in late 2013, Hardy apparently sent Wright an email congratulating him on becoming a billionaire. Hardy was able to calculate this because Wright had given him all the details of his wallet holdings. Wright had been completely open about what he had—to the extent that he had sent Hardy emails from the "Satoshi" email address as if to confirm his alter ego.

"He wanted them to know that this was as real as real could be real. They knew what was going on," Chesher says.

The enthusiasm for Wright's idea was short-lived, however. Not everyone at the tax office was as enthusiastic about Wright's idea as Michael Hardy had been.

"One day, this guy who was head of legal, one of those dandies in a pink striped shirt and a bow tie, walked in. He sat down and said quite calmly 'This is not going to happen. It will never happen that we recognize Bitcoin as a currency in Australia. In fact we recognize it as an asset and we're going to chase you for tax on that asset,'" Chesher explains.

Before long, the relationship between the ATO and Wright became toxic to the extent that Wright felt that their attitude had become personally motivated. And he may have had a valid point. On a dime, Wright's conversations with the tax office went from being positive to perilous. Simultaneously, the boss, Des McMaster, who previously had been the superior of the tax agent Wright had triumphed over at the tribunal saw an opportunity to get the guy who had done his man, so to speak. The way it looked was that there was a score to settle and all of the above led to both angry exchanges between Wright and the ATO, and appropriately spiraling legal bills being accrued and carried by Clayton Utz, the law firm who represented Wright's company.

"Where things got to, was in my opinion, nothing more than a personal vendetta against Craig by several high-ranking officers in the Australian Tax Office," Stefan Matthews says.

"What caused that level of animosity, I'm not sure. I know Craig had a history with the ATO dating back several years—again involving Bitcoin. That ended up either in court or in administrative appeals. Craig won, and I believe there was some animosity there because of that. And then when Craig's file started to land on some desks again, I guess it opened the door for them to throw a few knives in to see if they could bring the whole house of cards down," he added.

"Des was a really nasty piece of work," John Chesher says. "This was undoubtedly personal. He was very polite and smarmy on the surface and at first he sent in one of his young assistants to talk to us about this and that. Then at the end of it they all came back with jackboots on, figuratively speaking. Looking back, I think that somewhere along the line they'd had directives from the US about Bitcoin. And when the US says jump, Australia says, how high? They did a full one-eighty. From that point it was incredible to watch how quickly things changed and became very aggressive."

Regardless, Wright continued to apply for research grant approvals via the Australian Government's AusIndustry program and later filing reimbursement claims associated with this research and development—all perfectly above board. Although Wright had filed claims correctly and had apparently always collaborated with the many audits his business was exposed to over the years, it wasn't enough to hold the tax office at bay.

There came a point in late 2014, where they put the brakes on everything and wanted to launch an in-depth investigation into Wright's companies' activities. Without these valuable claim refunds, Wright was running on fumes. The likely trigger was that Wright's reimbursement claim numbers had been going through the roof year on year and the tax office had been increasingly getting tense as a result. Wright's company and its various subsidiaries had been spending vast sums on research and development which, amongst other things, included the construction—reputedly in collaboration with a US-based tech company called SGI—of complex and astronomically expensive super-computers required to power his research in the area of Bitcoin scaling.

Meanwhile, the Australian Tax Office simply couldn't get a handle on what, if any, income was being generated to offset such vast outlay. They started to suspect that his R&D claims were nothing more than a front for fraud. One way or another, they wanted to take Craig Wright down.

Twenty-fifteen was to be a monumental year in the history of Bitcoin, but it began as inauspiciously as it could possibly have.

Within a month or so of the turn of the year, there were a number of pressure points threatening to choke the life out of Wright's business activities in Australia. The primary problem was working capital—specifically that Wright's company, DeMorgan Ltd., was running out of it and doing so alarmingly fast.

In the absence of claim reimbursements, DeMorgan had been funding its day-to-day operations throughout the previous year by either liquidating bitcoin to cash or paying for goods and services with bitcoin itself. These were Wright's own coins, but not the so-called 'Satoshi 'coins apparently—which couldn't be accessed simply because by that point Wright had not been unmasked as being Satoshi Nakamoto and therefore to have used them would have blown his cover.

The exact origin of these coins is still unclear, however. In the author Andrew O'Hagan's 2016 article for *London Review of Books* about his time in Wright's world, it is suggested that these actually *were* Satoshi coins that were used, up to 650,000 of them, with the remainder held in a trust in Seychelles. This aforementioned trust—the Tulip Trust—was first referenced in email communication between Wright and Dave Kleiman in 2011, in information later revealed to the public by *WIRED* and *Gizmodo*.

Again, the basis of the trust, if the trust existed at all in material terms, was that Kleiman and other unnamed trustees were given custody of approximately 1.1 million bitcoin to put into the trust until January 2020 whereupon they would revert to Wright. What was significant was that apparently, in the interim, there was provision that Wright could be loaned bitcoin in order to further his research and development activity.

"These were not Satoshi coins I was using; I received $20 million from a 1999 listing and was using the proceeds from that," Wright says, presumably referring to the work he conducted for

Lasseters Casino. "I created gaming software solutions and other products and was paid for that.

When pressed further, Wright explained that some or all—he never actually said which—of that $20 million had been used to purchase coins via the Russian WMIRK digital currency exchange using another digital currency called Liberty Reserve Dollars, a defunct form of cryptocurrency associated with a company called Liberty Reserve that operated out of Costa Rica as an asset exchange.

While the US Government would ultimately seize and shut down Liberty Reserve in 2013 amid claims it was handling billions of criminal proceeds, Wright said he had merely purchased these coins as an investment in 2011, with no plans to access them.

Other suggestions that these coins, purchased in February of that year, were in some way associated with the now infamous Mt. Gox exchange hack where hundreds of thousands of bitcoin were "lost," the details of which only came to light three years later in 2014, appear to be unsubstantiated. In fact, the only piece of evidence linking Wright's "1 Feex" (so called simply because the wallet address began with those five digits) Bitcoin wallet address to the Mt. Gox hack at all is an alleged Skype text dialogue between the exchange's founder Jed McCaleb and its soon-to-be purchaser, French developer Mark Karpeles, who would ultimately face charges years later of falsifying data to inflate the value of the exchange's holdings.

Whatever the specifics of where Wright's working capital came from—and one of the themes of this story is that cast iron facts like this are often hard to come by—what matters is that one way or another Wright had been staying afloat.

In fact, up until late 2014 DeMorgan had been running an office with forty-five or so staff in the Sydney suburb of North Ryde, continuing to conduct Bitcoin and blockchain related research documentation and project management. It was cutting edge work at the fast-evolving frontier of technology.

As 2014 was turning to 2015, things began getting really desperate. Wright's business interests—and there was a complex web of companies that it encompassed—was in a state of operational meltdown and one was already in administration. Wright and his new wife Ramona, whom he'd met in 2010 and married in 2013, had already sold their cars and it had reached a point where it had limited access to funds to pay staff and keep the lights on.

The ATO hadn't just put a hold on all of Wright's claims but they were also issuing crippling penalties on the basis that they felt his company's claims were suspect. Meanwhile, his lawyers, Clayton Utz, were sitting with an outstanding legal bill of something in the region of $1.2 million Australian dollars. In the middle of the firestorm was Craig Wright: tapped out financially, being scrutinized by the ATO at every turn—and with his own lawyers refusing to do further work on his behalf until a significant portion of the outstanding amount got paid.

The only glimmer of hope was that Andrew Sommer, a partner at the law firm, was digging in to fight what looked like a lone battle on Wright's behalf. He seemingly liked him, knew all about his invention, and indeed had been representing him since prior to the beginning of Bitcoin. But even his loyalty to Wright had its limits. Despite Sommer's support, other partners at Clayton Utz, who coincidentally also represented the Australian Tax Office, were far less sympathetic and seemingly encouraged Sommer to tow the company line. Wright's combative attitude did not help his cause.

"Craig basically thought they were being dicks," Stefan Matthews suggests. "And, typical of Craig, he had no problem telling them that."

Wright felt that, because he'd paid his lawyers millions in fees over the years, $1.2 million shouldn't be too much debt to carry. The partners disagreed and some wanted to drop him as a client altogether, citing a potential conflict of interest. All in all, it was a deteriorating situation with no obvious solution in sight.

As if the financial outlook wasn't bad enough, there were other equally pressing concerns of a different nature for someone whose involvement with the invention of Bitcoin was not yet in the public domain.

Not only had there been longstanding rumors that some of Wright's staff, disgruntled, jealous, or otherwise, had been stealing intellectual property and attempting to either sell it or planning to go off and do something with it themselves for their own profit, there was also a suggestion that some had been plotting against him or even colluding with his many enemies—including, perhaps, hackers. These warning signs dated back to the latter part of the previous year.

"My theory is that, when the ATO were looking into Craig's tax stuff in 2013 and 2014, there were people inside of Craig's organization who were working with the ATO, and by extension, also working with Ira Kleiman," Kurt Wuckert Jr., Bitcoin Historian at *CoinGeek* explains.

"I think people wanted to either blackmail Craig or leak his information. Why? I think it's highly likely that Craig had done work for the CIA and / or Homeland Security at some point. So when the ATO contacted these agencies and said they're investigating an Australian guy for tax issues and want access to some files, what are these agencies going to do? They're going to hire a skilled engineer to unwind it all. And there were only half a dozen people in the world at that time who had the ability to do it," Wuckert continues.

Sure enough, in September of 2014, some of the email accounts belonging to Satoshi Nakamoto had indeed been hacked, with the hacker posting messages to SourceForge and the P2P Foundation forum threatening to sell information online for twenty-five bit-coin—the equivalent of $11,000 at the time. Satoshi was being blackmailed publicly. Email history—and who knows what else dating back as far as late 2008—had fallen into unfriendly hands.

"Dear Satoshi," the message read. "Your dox, passwords and IP addresses are being sold on the darknet. Apparently you didn't configure Tor properly and your IP leaked when you used your email account sometime in 2010. You are not safe. You need to get out of where you are as soon as possible before these people harm you. Thank you for inventing Bitcoin."

Wright, of course, would have been fully aware of the hack's implications. The noose in his own mind would have only tightened.

"At this point, Craig would have known he was burned. He had to have known," Wuckert reckons. "Imagine your worst enemy having access to your sent emails from the last five years."

"I was in Australia at the time of the gmx hack," Wright recalls. "Basically it was arseholes trying to extort money out of me—yet again. And they didn't get it. Did some of the information in those emails ultimately filter back to the people who ultimately outed me? Probably. But there was also a lot of stuff in there that has never come out and they presumably didn't like and didn't want out: my opinions on how Bitcoin should work, scale and so on. They wanted that covered up. But I also think—and I found this out for sure much later—that Ira Kleiman was somehow involved too. He'd been trying to insert himself into my story for some time with a view to ultimately suing me," Wright continues.

As for his involvement with the CIA, this also appears to be true.

"I did some forensic and incident work in the past. I did so on and off from the mid-'90s up until around 2011. I was what they called a 'suitcase man,'" Wright explains. "Jarheads have a habit of blowing things up, so I had to go out to locations and secure computer systems and even phones. Hard drives that have bullets fired through them don't tend to work very well."

Regardless of what he felt about his email history being accessed, which, incidentally, would have made it crystal clear to any would-be hacker that he was indeed the person behind the Satoshi pseudonym, in late 2014, Wright had been more focused on his immediate cash flow pressures and keeping his research and development endeavors afloat and the IP secure. He also felt considerable responsibility for the livelihoods of his staff.

In December of 2014, Wright contacted Stefan Matthews, who by that time had left Centrebet after they'd been sold to their rival Sportingbet and had then taken up a role in London working for Bodog UK, which was owned by Calvin Ayre. Matthews remained in London for a year before relocating back to the Philippines. It was while Matthews was back in Manila that he heard from Wright out of the blue around Christmas of 2014.

Wright had heard via a mutual friend that Matthews was going to be in Australia for the New Year's Eve firework celebrations at Sydney Harbour. Wright suggested they grab a beer.

"I'd lost contact with Craig for a few years, but only because I'd been embroiled in a long period of boardroom discussions about selling the business before I left Australia and moved to London. I don't think I was in touch with him at all but I did periodically hear what he was up to via a mutual friend of ours," Matthews recalls.

On the late morning of January 2nd, 2015, Wright and his wife Ramona met with Matthews for a social catch-up in the lobby restaurant of the Harbour View Hotel in North Sydney. No beer was consumed. Instead, they had a hamburger each and a couple of Cokes and discussed their respective lives, touched on what was going on with Bitcoin, its survival and growth, then shook hands and parted ways.

"It was only when I was in the elevator later that night that it occurred to me that our meeting had no purpose whatsoever. Furthermore, I had no more interest in Craig's Bitcoin stuff then than I'd ever had. I hadn't even Googled it since Craig first mentioned it to me years earlier," Matthews explained.

In what would later prove to be a fortunate twist of fate, not long after the January 2015 meeting Matthews left the gambling industry in search of new challenges. After spending ten days with Calvin Ayre in Antigua ruminating about his future, they agreed that Matthews would return to Manila to work out of an office of the Sterling Group, an Ayre-owned Venture Capital Company. Here he would be focused on looking out for non-gaming tech-related investment opportunities in the region on which he and Ayre might collaborate going forward. If gaming opportunities came across his desk, of course he'd pass them on to Ayre's gaming group.

But betting and gaming were no longer the focus for Matthews. After ten years at the coalface of that uniquely cutthroat industry, he was looking for something new and exciting, perhaps even a legacy project to ease himself toward retirement. If Craig Wright and Bitcoin was the Holy Grail he was seeking, Matthews still didn't know it. Regardless, in April of 2015, Wright again contacted Matthews and suggested they set up another meeting.

"I need your help," Wright told his friend explicitly on the phone.

"Why me?" Matthews asked.

"Because you're the only person in the world that I trust, who will understand, and whom I believe will give me sensible advice that I'm likely to follow," Wright told him.

From Wright, that was high praise indeed.

"What do you want to do?" Matthews asked him. "What do you *want*?" he added, while staring directly into the center of Wright's soul down the telephone line.

It was the magic question, and Wright had the answer.

"I don't want to run a business anymore," Wright began. "I just want to create. I want to create for the rest of my life, and I want other people to run businesses and other people to take my creations and do important things with them," he continued.

Matthews knew he had to be in Sydney to sign some legal papers, so the two agreed to meet again, with two colleagues of Wright's, Allan Pedersen and Dr. Stephanae Savanah, present.

The plan was for them to lay Craig Wright's predicament out on the table, warts and all—and also to present Stefan Matthews with a comprehensive overview of the kind of research and development work DeMorgan and its staff had been conducting in the area of blockchain and IP.

"When I started working for Craig's Sydney companies, I was officially employed by one of the many interconnected companies called 'Integyrz'—an online education entity. At that stage, I had not heard of Bitcoin. After some structuring, I was transferred to DeMorgan in the summer of 2015 and it was clear to me that the relationship between Craig and the ATO was vexatious," Dr. Stephanae Savanah says, "I also knew that that enmity existed between Craig and certain high-ranking officials at the ATO and I was working on rewriting the text of DeMorgan's applications for R&D rebates," Savanah continues.

The meeting the next day revealed that Wright was looking to Matthews for sage advice, but more than that, he was also grasping for a financial lifeline. First and foremost, Wright needed to clear his feet of the debt owed to Clayton Utz. Without that sizeable burden being addressed, nothing else could happen. DeMorgan was staring into the abyss. Bankruptcy loomed.

However, in the face of this huge pressure, Wright wasn't lying down. He had seemingly approached Macquarie Bank for a loan and from all reports they had been forthcoming in principle. They were apparently willing to inject $10 million into Wright's businesses, but with certain conditions. First, they wanted a full audit done by KPMG out of Melbourne. Second, they wanted rights to Wright's research and intellectual property, in addition to insisting on a stake in any future sales of Wright's IPO.

"Craig said to me, 'You know what cunts they are, once they've got their claws into me, I won't own anything anymore,'" Matthews explains.

"I had never even considered commercializing my research," Craig says. "I could get the money, that wasn't the problem. It was more a question of whether I wanted a bank controlling this commercialization that was the question. To me, my intellectual property was always more important than the money anyway. It was my life."

Although Macquarie Bank's proposal was a viable get-out-of-financial-jail card for Wright, it still represented a less than appealing last resort. As much as he might have wanted to work for someone else, "working" for a bank—because that's how he saw the relationship playing out—wasn't the road he wanted to go down.

"If it wasn't for Stefan, I might not have had a choice," Wright admits. "He was the only person I trusted enough."

After the meeting, Wright and Matthews agreed to meet later for dinner. Matthews, meanwhile, returned to his hotel room, sat down on the bed, and pulled out his laptop. Into a Google search he typed "Bitcoin" and after clicking around for a while he found himself staring at Satoshi Nakamoto's white paper.

"The hairs on the back of my neck stood up," Matthews remembers. "It suddenly dawned on me that I'd seen the document before. And the reason I had was because Craig had had a hard copy with him in my Centrebet office back in 2008. And he handed a USB stick to me from which I printed my own copy."

"There's something I've got to ask you," Matthews said to Wright as their dinner engagement later that evening wound down. "Who the fuck is Satoshi Nakamoto?"

"You already know the answer to that…" Wright replied, staring back at Matthews across the table.

Irritated by Wright's deflecting non-answer, Matthews pushed harder.

"Come on, Craig. I'm not in the mood for games. I'm asking you a direct question and I'd appreciate a straight answer."

"You're looking at him," Wright calmly replied.

Matthews then told Wright that he had now connected the dots between the USB he'd been given and the white paper he'd read the evening prior. "I knew I'd seen it before," he told Wright. As Matthews explained his thought process, Wright held a hand up to stop his friend mid flow and then explained that, actually, he was incorrect.

The version he had shown to Matthews in July 2008 was not the final white paper, Wright told him. It was in fact two versions *removed* from the white paper that was finally published in October that year. Wright also confirmed to Matthews that it was his late friend Dave Kleiman who had been responsible for the editing that was applied to the document in order to "make it all more readable."

The two men then discussed Wright's early days of mining bitcoin in the cattle shed of his farm in the New South Wales countryside, his reasoning behind the Satoshi Nakamoto pseudonym, and the extent of the research that had been undertaken since Satoshi stepped away from day-to-day public Bitcoin conversation in 2010. Wright also reminded Matthews of the offer he'd proposed in 2009 to exchange $500 dollars for 50,000 bitcoin, which at the time had next to no value. It seems certain that these would indeed have been so-called "Satoshi" coins, with addresses associated to the mining of blocks in early 2009 during the first three months of the blockchain's existence.

The significance of these coins did not register with Matthews at all. Because of his general disinterest in Bitcoin at the time, and because he also doubted his own ability to look after the private keys to coins of any kind, Matthews turned Wright's offer away, suggesting that Bitcoin was just another in a long list of clever initiatives that was ultimately doomed to failure. In his years in the gambling industry he'd seen plenty of them before. Now, in 2015, however, Wright was having the last laugh.

"I bet you wish you'd taken me up on that deal now," Wright told Matthews.

"If you were any sort of a cunt you'd still give them to me!" Matthews replied, by that time sufficiently clued-in to know that the bitcoin price sat at somewhere in excess of $200 each.

"I did the math," says Matthews. "And he never did give me them," he adds.

The two parted ways, and with his mind in a combined state of bewilderment and excitement, Matthews flew back to Manila to digest everything he'd just heard and to think what to do about it. During the flight, Matthews reflected on his personal history with Wright, and how, for whatever reason, the man, much like a boomerang, kept coming back.

"I've had fucking thousands of people in my life," Matthews told me. "Many of them I drifted away from and never heard from again. But Craig was this personality that just kept re-appearing, and always for different reasons. It wasn't that either one of us was particularly clamoring after the other for affection or companionship; it was a variety of unrelated circumstances over a number of years that kept bringing this fucker back into my life."

Matthews also had time to consider some of the business propositions Wright had brought into focus via the conversations that took place in the meeting attended by Wright's two colleagues where Matthews was given chapter and verse details about exactly what DeMorgan and its staff had been doing in their Sydney office in the area of the blockchain.

"Only then, for the first time, did I really start to think about what all this blockchain technology that underpinned Bitcoin was all about. That was a huge turning point in my life. It was at that moment that I realized that I had overlooked something really profound and fundamentally important back in 2008," Matthews explains. "I kicked myself because I don't normally overlook things. But I wouldn't change anything. Things happen for a reason."

On further reflection, Matthews also admitted to himself that the reason he'd repeatedly batted away an opportunity that had been staring him in the face wasn't the idea itself, but the messenger: Craig Steven Wright.

"Craig was always talking about it and always wanting to spend time with me explaining it all. But I just didn't have that time. I had a business to run and we were also in the midst of talking to, at boardroom level, potential acquirers of that business," Matthews recalls. "So it wasn't that I didn't like Craig. I did like the guy and I knew he was fucking smart. But I found his conversations—sitting down and chewing the fat with him about topics that weren't of value to me day-to-day—an imposition on my time," he continued.

On the return flight to Manila, Matthews made a decision that would alter his destiny. He promised himself that, as long as blockchain technology was around and available, he wanted it to be central to everything he did.

This—April of 2015—was the turning point where Craig Steven Wright transitioned from being an occasional friend to being a major influence on Stefan Matthews's life. At the age of almost sixty, perhaps he had found his legacy project.

CHAPTER **FIVE**

Summit

"**A**re you sitting down?" Matthews asked Calvin Ayre when he called him at his Vancouver penthouse. With the relative time differences, he'd waited less than twelve hours since returning from his life-changing meeting with Craig Wright to make the call.

"What's up?' Ayre replied, curious.

"Well…" started Matthews. "I've got one hell of a story to tell you. Do you know what Bitcoin is?"

"Yes."

"Do you know who Satoshi Nakamoto is?"

"No," Ayre replied.

"Well, I do," Matthews told him. "You've got to meet this guy."

"Ya? Keep talking," Ayre said.

Matthews then embarked on a long tale about his history with Craig Wright over the years and how gifted he was; the white paper he'd seen and largely ignored in 2008; and how it had suddenly dawned on him sitting in a Sydney hotel room, that Wright, the human boomerang who'd been in and out of his life for ten years, was none other than Satoshi Nakamoto, the inventor of Bitcoin.

At the end of the conversation, Matthews also touched on—without going into too much unnecessary detail—some of the difficulties Wright was having in Australia. He also lightly pitched the idea of Bitcoin and blockchain technology potentially being the kind of VC project they'd been looking for and left it at that.

"I want to hear more. What's the next step?" Ayre said.

"I think Craig and I should fly over and I'll introduce you and the three of us should talk," Matthews told him. "Let's just see where it leads."

Matthews saw Ayre as one of his closest allies, as both a friend and a business colleague whose judgement he trusted implicitly. Even so, he had no expectation of the idea amounting to anything. "Calvin could have easily met Craig and thought he was a raving nutcase," Matthews recalls.

At this point in 2015, Calvin Ayre was still trapped between Antigua and Canada, flying back and forth between the two on private planes and staying out of the United States altogether, on the advice of his lawyers.

"I was basically stuck," Ayre explains. "But I was definitely looking for a project, something that I could sink my teeth into once I was freed up from the Americans. I just didn't know when that would be."

Fortunately, because of his gambling industry background, Ayre's knowledge of Bitcoin and blockchain technology was already extensive relative to what was publicly available at that time.

"Everybody had been tinkering with it for payment systems right from the start. And you have to remember that, at the beginning, what we now call BTC actually was a viable low cost, peer-to-peer payments platform," Ayre says. "As such, it would have been impossible not to know about it in my industry."

Wright and Matthews flew separately to Vancouver from Sydney and Manila respectively, and arrived there an hour apart on Sunday June 7th, 2015.

The two got situated, then left their hotel, The Opus on Davie Street, and went for dinner and a couple of drinks at the Cactus

Club Café in Yaletown, a hip and happening neighborhood on the south side of the downtown Vancouver peninsula synonymous with converted warehouses and swish cocktail bars and stylish restaurants.

The following morning, Matthews took Wright to meet Calvin Ayre at his penthouse at 283 Davie Street, which had a large deck that overlooked the corner of Davie and Pacific. Wright was introduced to Ayre, the three talked, and then they all wandered down the road to a local restaurant for lunch before returning to talk further on the deck.

"It was kind of funny," Matthews remembers. "During the morning, Calvin leaned over to me at one point and said: 'Is it okay if I ask him if he's Satoshi Nakamoto?' 'Fuck yeah,' I told him. 'Ask him anything you want.'"

Sure enough, sometime mid-afternoon, by which time a few bottles of red wine had been consumed in the June sunshine on Ayre's deck, Wright returned from the bathroom and Matthews set up the burning question Ayre desperately wanted to ask.

"Figuratively speaking, I put the ball on a tee, handed Calvin a big golf club, and invited him to smack it," Matthews recalls.

"Oi, Craig. Calvin's actually got a question for you…" Matthews said.

With that, Ayre looked at Wright, fixed his piercing sea-blue eyes upon his new acquaintance, and said, "I hope you're not offended if I ask this," Ayre began. "But are you really Satoshi Nakamoto?"

Before Wright responded, Ayre was at pains to explain to Wright that the reason he was asking wasn't because he doubted him per se, but more because he just wanted to hear it in his own words.

"He confirmed to me that he was, and he did it in a way that was almost childlike, like a kid admitting something he was sheepish about but also proud of," Ayre recalls.

The two talked and Wright explained to Ayre the entire trajectory of Bitcoin up until the present day, all of which answered Ayre's burning question to his satisfaction. As far as Ayre was concerned, he was in the company of Satoshi Nakamoto, the legendary inventor of Bitcoin.

"As I watched them interact," Matthews recalls, "It was like me watching how I first got to know Calvin when I first met him in 2010. Up until that point I'd heard of him and I admired Bodog, but we'd never actually met. When we did, it was one of those significant moments and Calvin has said the same thing. There was no courtship; we just clicked. Watching Craig was a mirror image. Calvin and Craig understood each other and gelled straightaway, just as Calvin and I had."

The Vancouver "summit" meeting was momentous by any measurement. One way or another, Bitcoin's integrity was going to be saved because of it. Indeed, the collision of these three individuals, all with differing but invaluable attributes, was to be the foundation point of a decision to both salvage Craig Wright's faltering business and also to seize back control of Satoshi Nakamoto's original Bitcoin protocol, just as it had been envisioned in the white paper seven years previously.

"I liked Craig when I met him. Talking to him face to face really helped me connect the dots in my head about how the technology worked," Ayre reflects. "I didn't know exactly how it—a deal—was all going to work, but I knew that Bitcoin and blockchain was something I wanted to be involved with even though I still had reservations about exactly how involved I could be."

To that extent, Monday June 8th, 2015 is a date that will forever be etched in history as when the process of saving Bitcoin began in earnest.

There was, however, still much work to be done. The bones of their first notional conversations were just bones. Now they needed some meat.

Buoyed by the previous day's positivity, the three men sprang out of bed early Tuesday morning. After spit-balling ideas over breakfast, a decision was made to try to set up a visit to the offices of nTrust—a company headquartered in Vancouver and known to Calvin Ayre.

According to publicly available information, nTrust—part of nChain Holdings—was founded in 2011 and operated primarily in the remittance corridor connecting Canada and the Philippines, where the company also retained an office. Also, according to company records, it was ostensibly a tech outfit focusing on start-up ventures, financial services, and Bitcoin, and it employed roughly thirty people.

The reasoning behind the visit to nTrust was that Matthews and Ayre had privately discussed what some of the next steps might be for potential funding, and one suggestion they both agreed upon was to introduce Wright to Robert MacGregor, an IP lawyer by trade and the main man at nTrust. The intention initially was to establish if there was any synergy between what nTrust were doing and what Wright had been working on in Australia for the preceding five years.

"Stefan had told me about Robert MacGregor sometime back toward the end of 2014. There was some email back and forth and a five-minute call," Craig Wright remembers. "At that time it was because nTrust were doing similar things and I had some entities that might have been of a help to them. Had those conversations gone any further, things would look very different to what they do now. But Rob thought too much of himself and I probably thought too much of myself at that time for anything to develop."

"I had known MacGregor for several years," Matthews says. "Calvin had also known him for a few years, because, in his capacity as an IP lawyer, he'd done some things in and around the gaming space. I can't remember exactly how, but I had heard that he was trying to set up electronic payment systems between Canada and the Philippines to reduce costs. I didn't know where he was at with it all, but I suggested to Calvin that we all might meet in person."

Matthews was given the green light to set something up. He made a phone call to nTrust and got a message to CBO Rod Hsu to enquire if the three men could stop in for a meeting at their office—a concrete and glass affair located at 1045 Howe Street in downtown Vancouver.

As it turned out, the man they specifically wanted to see in person, Robert MacGregor, wasn't in town. Nevertheless, an appointment was made, and Wright, Ayre, and Matthews jumped in a cab and went across town to the nTrust office for the agreed time and shortly afterwards found themselves sitting around a table in a meeting room.

"There was the three of us and three or four of their employees that included Rod Hsu and COO Angela Reiner," Matthews recalls. "And then part way through the meeting, MacGregor appeared on a screen on the wall by video call from wherever he was in the world at that time."

By any measurement, this meeting at nTrust on June 8th was a little bizarre and strained, to put it mildly. Craig Wright was sitting there in his three-piece suit and tie while everyone else, consistent with laid-back tech-house culture, was in jeans, jogging pants, and t-shirts. MacGregor meanwhile, from his vantage point staring back from a screen on the wall, was seemingly a little blindsided and unaware as to why he'd even been asked to join.

As the conversations progressed, it became apparent that one of nTrust's ongoing missions was to endeavor to create a blockchain of their own that could compete with Bitcoin. Apparently, they'd taken the venture as far as filing a couple of patent applications for specific ideas around this area of research and development. It was also disclosed in the discussions at the table that the development had been put on temporary hold for one reason or another. Faced with these revelations, and perhaps a little affronted by the realization that someone was daring to challenge his invention, Craig Wright's ears pricked up.

"Craig started asking lots of questions about the design of their 'private' blockchain idea," Matthews remembers. "The guy said, 'you're asking technical questions. I think it would be best if we brought our CTO into the meeting.'" With that, nTrust's CTO Rino Ong was summoned to join the conversation.

"Okay, so why am I here?" Ong said when he sat down.

It was explained to Ong why the three strangers were there and that they were interested in hearing more specifics about nTrust's blockchain aspirations. What followed was seemingly an awkward standoff between Ong and Wright, a pissing contest of sorts between tech-heads.

"Craig started asking questions again and it got to a point in the conversation where the CTO was getting very defensive," Matthews remembers. "And Craig just kept asking more and more detailed questions."

Wright was essentially scrutinizing the integrity of nTrust's design idea. "If you're designing things the way you say you are, it won't work," was the long and short of Wright's assessment. Wright then asked a very specific question related to the architecture of the nTrust blockchain's protocol.

"The guy looked at Craig from directly across the table and said, 'Craig, I could answer that question for you but it's a bit technical. It might be over your head," Matthews remembers. "*Oh fuck no*, I thought."

Before anyone else could speak, Wright bristled visibly. In an instant, he went from a relaxed seated position, arms folded, to leaning forward, hands flat on the table, and staring straight back at the CTO. "It's okay," he began. "You can give me the answer in machine code if you prefer. I *read* machine code."

At that point, Calvin Ayre intervened. "Well, I think we're done here!" he said, jumping up from his seat at the table.

With that, the three amigos left the meeting and returned to Ayre's penthouse. Within moments of leaving nTrust, Matthews's phone was already ringing in his pocket. Seeing Robert MacGregor's name staring back at him from the iPhone screen, Matthews answered straightaway.

"What the fuck was all that about?" MacGregor said, clearly unimpressed by what he felt was a thinly veiled ambush.

Matthews de-escalated, briefly explained Wright's background and the reason for the impromptu meeting and left it at that. The two agreed to talk again.

As much as there was an "in-principle" willingness to work together going forward forged in Vancouver, it wasn't going to be easy to pull the pieces of a Craig Wright rescue package together quickly. Furthermore, the clock was ticking fast Down Under, a momentum driven by a combination of the tax office's aggressive actions and Clayton Utz's discomfort about the outstanding legal bill. With no money to address either of these issues, whatever was going to happen needed to happen fast.

"The bank wanted to give us five days," Wright recalls. "Then they said they were going to start pulling all our accounts. All of this was being done so that DeMorgan would go downhill and then the bank could come in and steal what we had by way of our IP, as they'd previously done with an idea of mine called white paper

32. At the time, I couldn't sue them until the patent was actually granted, which can take years," he added.

Wright had every reason to be stressed by his predicament and it was agreed that he would return to Australia immediately to prepare for due diligence ahead of some kind of potential bailout deal that the money men—Ayre and Matthews—could be working on at warp speed in the background.

"I gave him his marching orders," Ayre recalls, who then departed to a wellness retreat at the top of a mountain somewhere near Vernon, BC. The trip was meant to be relaxing and rejuvenating. The reality was anything but.

"I got a bit of a longwinded call from Craig. In fact, it was one of the most tortuous phone calls I've ever had. It had the opposite effect than what Craig was trying to do. I came away thinking he was deranged." Ayre recalls, "But I now know he was just distraught because he was running out of time."

Matthews, meanwhile, returned to Manila prior to traveling to Australia to spend a week becoming thoroughly acquainted with the minutiae of Wright's business affairs.

"Calvin also said that I should probably call Rob MacGregor again to fill him in more on the background, sooner rather than later," Matthews remembers.

MacGregor, however, beat him to the punch.

The Saturday afternoon following his return from Vancouver—June 13th—Matthews was sitting watching the live AFL game on the Australia channel in his home in Manila. Ten minutes into the broadcast his phone buzzed and on it was a message from MacGregor that read something to the effect of "we probably need to talk because I still need a full explanation."

"He was in Vancouver. I asked him when he wanted to talk," Matthews recalls. "And Rob replied saying that he wanted to talk right now. I thought *fuck! The footie is on....*"

Matthews turned the television off and connected with Robert MacGregor via Skype. MacGregor was seemingly still a little agitated by what had transpired the previous week. His staff had apparently been grilling him, asking what the background to the meeting was and who these people were that had descended upon the office out of nowhere. These were answers that he simply did not have. MacGregor went as far as to say that Wright, Ayre, and Matthews's antics amounted to disrupting the work of his staff and he was not happy about it.

"I think I said to him, 'Rob, for me to explain this to you will require me to tell you a long story,'" Matthews recalls.

"Yeah? Well I've got all the time you need," MacGregor apparently responded.

Matthews recounted more or less the same tale as he'd told Calvin Ayre a month or so prior. He talked for several minutes. At the other end there was only silence.

"It got to the point where I had to check if the call was even still connected and it was," Matthews laughs. "McGregor said absolutely nothing. I'm not even sure he was breathing. When I had finished telling him the story, we found ourselves in that situation they describe in the classics: 'whoever speaks next loses,' or whatever it is."

After what seemed like an eternity, MacGregor broke the silence and what he said was hardly the answer Matthews had been hoping for.

"I find all of this very hard to believe," he told Matthews.

Matthews explained to MacGregor that he could understand how the Wright and Satoshi Nakamoto story was a hard one to believe. He then went on to say that he wasn't even asking him to believe it all. He was merely telling him the situation as it was, and by extension why he and Wright had been in Vancouver to talk to Calvin Ayre in the first place.

"I told Rob that I was going to go down to Sydney and stay there for a while," says Matthews. "And I also told him that while I was down there I was going to take a deep dive into all things within the DeMorgan group. I wanted to discover and understand what the intellectual property was, what shape it was all in."

As much as Wright had briefed Matthews as to the dire state of his business affairs in April, and as fully as he'd also described the lay of the land to both he and Ayre in Vancouver, Stefan Matthews, an experienced business-man familiar with due diligence, still wanted to see and smell it all for himself.

"I suggested to MacGregor that he should also come down and overlap with me in Sydney" Matthews says. "But he said no."

Undeterred, on June 17th, Matthews boarded a flight to Sydney and checked himself into the Rydges North Sydney Hotel on McLaren Street. His reservation was for two weeks. He hoped that would be long enough.

Matthews hit the ground running. Right off the bat he set up a meeting with Andrew Sommer at Clayton Utz to establish the exact situation with both the outstanding legal bill and Wright's current position with the tax office. Thereafter, he immersed himself in the mire of paperwork and files that was DeMorgan's affairs, while at the same time keeping in regular contact with MacGregor back in Canada as he went.

"When I dug into it all, it looked to me as if Craig had been following the correct procedures," Stefan Matthews recalls of his first impressions of the DeMorgan paperwork.

"To file a claim, you needed to, in the first instance, go through a government department called AusIndustry to file a statement that showed what your research was. If they approved it as compliant research eligible for a rebate, it went through. And that's what Craig had been doing. I'm guessing there were at least twenty-five or thirty submissions made and they all came back with approval

95

and a number to be quoted in order to reclaim the rebates. The tax office had nothing to do with approving or disapproving R&D. They only issue the rebates against AusIndustry approved research. They looked at some of the claims and said, 'How did you pay for this in the first place?' to which Craig must have said, 'Well, I paid it using bitcoin.' To them that wasn't acceptable and that's where it all fell over," Matthews continues.

Sometime during the first week, perhaps out of curiosity because of Matthews's occasional check-ins, Robert MacGregor decided he too would fly to Sydney after all. He asked Matthews where he was staying and said he'd see him in a day or so. "He ended up staying not in my hotel, but in a hotel just around the corner," Matthews says laughing.

Matthews and MacGregor met for breakfast the morning after he arrived and the two talked about what Matthews had been doing. They then jumped in Matthews's rental car and made their way to DeMorgan's offices in North Ryde, a suburb in the north-west of Sydney.

"Along the way he kept saying things to me along the lines of 'I don't believe any of this' and 'I just can't get my head around it,'" Matthews remembers about the twenty-minute car journey along Sydney's Pacific Highway to meet Craig Wright.

Matthews and MacGregor arrived at an unremarkable building at 32 Delhi Road in North Ryde, which was the registered address of two of Wright's companies: DeMorgan Ltd. and Panopticrypt Pty Ltd. Wright's office, painted red, was a unit on the fifth floor and overlooked the local cemetery. At street level was a bustling coffee place, Delhi 32.

What they found in DeMorgan's office was essentially an evacuation site—a ghost town, with no staff, still open laptops on the desks, open books, and even printed pages still lying in photocopier trays. The only living things present in the building were Craig Wright, Allan Pederson, and his attorney Andrew Sommer.

"Craig told us that he had had to stand almost all of his staff down because he'd had no money to pay them for two or three weeks. Anyone who was still there was working for free," Matthews explains.

If the dire nature of Wright's predicament hadn't been evident from previous conversations, it certainly was now. With no money and now no staff, DeMorgan appeared as if it was on life support—if not straight up flatlining.

However, there was hope. A moment of pure chance was about to change the conversation—and by extension Craig Wright's luck—completely.

As Robert MacGregor and Stefan Matthews assessed the scale of the operation in front of them, they entered a room full of files, catalogued research, named binders, and endless documentation that had been created to support Wright's myriad of research and development claims that had been filed throughout the preceding years since before the birth of Bitcoin.

"There was a story going around that it was me who found documents relating to blockchains and white papers, etc.," Matthews recalls. "But it was actually Rob MacGregor who found it. He was poking around looking in storerooms, and at one point, he came to me and said, 'Have you seen this?' pointing into a room full of files."

"Have a look at this," MacGregor said to Matthews.

"There's fucking thousands of files in here. What is it that you want me to look at?" Matthews replied.

MacGregor pointed Matthews in the direction of an open lever arch file in which there was a document around a particular blockchain research topic.

"What's your point?" Matthews asked.

"Well, have a look at the date…" MacGregor replied. "It is dated 2006. It precedes the release of Bitcoin and the white paper. And it has Craig's name on it."

It was a pivotal discovery, the equivalent of pulling a four-leaf clover out of a haystack. It was at that point that Robert MacGregor's attitude and demeanor changed completely. Indeed, over the next couple of days he spoke more to Wright about exactly what it was he needed and at the same time set about drafting a term sheet that was ultimately signed on June 29th.

"It was funny," says Wright. "During these conversations with Rob, Stefan and Allan I said to him, 'Did you know I was Satoshi?' Allan said, 'Of course we did!' 'Why didn't you say anything?' I asked him, and he just said that everyone knew. I had no idea. I'd never considered what everyone thought."

Although Robert MacGregor was in the room when the deal was signed, his signature was not on the page. Seemingly, because the rescue package had been pulled together in a hurry to allow the Clayton Utz bill to be paid and for legal representation to resume, he was still deliberating as to how exactly his involvement would be structured.

"My name was on the term sheet in my capacity as Vice President of The Sterling Group, as were Craig's and Ramona's," Stefan Matthews says. "The Sterling Group was initially used only as a party to the agreement to allow it to move forward quickly until the transaction could be fully sorted. I think Rob wanted more time to determine which of his entities would be involved."

Regardless, a term sheet was signed amid collective sighs of relief. The celebration could begin.

"Craig went to his home, which was five minutes away, and returned with a bottle of expensive Krug 2009 champagne. But we didn't have any appropriate glasses so in the absence of anything better we just sat there drinking this expensive champagne out of coffee cups," Matthews remembers fondly.

Matthews and MacGregor shared a rental car back to their respective hotels in North Sydney. Only then did the gravity of their positions start to sink in.

"Do you know what you've just done?" MacGregor said, turning to Matthews.

"What do you mean?" Matthews enquired.

"People work all their fucking careers in MMA practices and they don't do deals of the significance of the one you've just put together," MacGregor replied.

"I don't see it that way," Matthews said.

"This is worth fucking millions, if not billions," MacGregor shot back.

CHAPTER **SIX**

Relocation

As the last drop of Krug champagne was going down in a Sydney office, on the other side of the world one of the saddest chapters in the wider world of Bitcoin had just drawn to a close.

By June 2015, when Craig Wright was signing a landmark deal to save his business and lifetime of work, perhaps the most famous of Bitcoin corruptions, the darknet site Silk Road saga where huge volumes of bitcoin were used to purchase everything illegal you can think of on an online black marketplace, had come and gone. Although it was far from the only site of this kind using bitcoin to facilitate nefarious practices online, Silk Road was, without a doubt, the most high-profile, and as such, it became symbolic as perhaps the nadir of the Bitcoin narrative to date. More importantly, grimy illegal acts were the antithesis of what Satoshi Nakamoto had envisioned for his prized creation.

But if Craig Wright could take any solace from the Silk Road story it was that at least his invention held up. After all, the inherent traceability of the blockchain system he had created had eventually been Silk Road's downfall. Indeed, when US authorities started looking into Silk Road, every transaction could be observed, and they duly were when the site was shut down by the FBI in October 2013. By late May of 2015, its alleged founder, Ross

Ulbricht, who had coincidentally moved to live with his sister in Sydney for six months in 2010 before starting Silk Road, had been handed a double life sentence plus forty years and was languishing in a prison in Tucson, AZ.

"I did meet Ross back in 2010," Wright reflects. "Some of my friends in Sydney were in the surfing community and I used to go to this place called the Bondi Icebergs Club where they all hung out. On one such occasion, Ross, a keen surfer, was also there and we did discuss Bitcoin, among many other things, over beers. I just didn't realize it all would end up in a drugs system. I should have guessed some of these people would fucking do it, though. I can't believe how daft people were for thinking Bitcoin was anonymous. And then on top of that was all the child pornography and grooming that nobody talked about. Kids were blackmailed."

As much as Silk Road tarnished Bitcoin's reputation and must have placed it, and significantly, its creator, firmly on US Law Enforcement's radar, Wright, still not "outed" publicly as Satoshi Nakamoto, at least had some wiggle room. All he could do was distance himself from the negative aspects of his creation and keep moving forward.

As such, the initial deal to rescue Wright and Bitcoin was ultimately brokered. To make such a deal work, a company had to be established in a yet to be decided jurisdiction and it was this company that would acquire all of the intellectual property that belonged to all of Wright's many companies in Australia, which, at that time, numbered sixteen. Also to be included in this package was all intellectual property relating to Bitcoin and blockchain technology that was owned by Wright personally.

The company that would ultimately fulfil these functions was called nCrypt, also part of nChain Holdings, and it was agreed—based on Calvin Ayre's insistence that London was where the best pool of research talent would likely be found—that a research center would be set up in London where Craig Wright would be installed as Chief Scientist, with no directorships or management responsibilities whatsoever. The company would later be rebranded, simply, nChain.

"London wasn't my first choice," Wright says. "We looked at places in Canada. I considered Edinburgh in Scotland, but my wife said it was too cold in winter and too dark. We ended up in London."

Flowing back the other way in the deal would be a series of payments that would not only allow the Clayton Utz bill to be paid off entirely, but also would fund DeMorgan's unlisted holding company sufficiently on a monthly basis to allow a basic staff to be rehired, some research to continue and also to comprehensively document the entire cache of research archive so that it could easily be transferred to nCrypt—a process that would be overseen by Byron Angelopulo at IP lawyers Baker McKenzie in Sydney and would stretch into late December 2015.

Not only that, it was also agreed that capital would be made available to fund DeMorgan's ongoing legal dispute with the ATO. Whether the end result was an outright DeMorgan win or some form of a settlement position—the money would be in place.

Beyond that, the plan was to work through any outstanding objections to DeMorgan's R&D claims in parallel with the establishment of the London office of what would late become nChain.

Ultimately, Craig Wright would have his wishes granted. Although he'd retain property in Australia, he'd be primarily living in London with his wife Ramona and family by his side.

His first employment contact was executed with an entity called Tyche and the application for a UK sponsored employment visa was filed on his behalf. Once nChain Ltd. was fully set up, Wright's and several other members of staff's employment contracts would be transferred over.

RELOCATION

On a daily basis Wright would be in his element: holed up in a bright and airy West End office conducting the research he loved so much in a frenetic blur of pen and whiteboard. At his disposal would be a skilled support team to work as a conduit between him and an external patent attorney who'd then identify and file block-chain related patents.

At it stood in June of 2015, the plan wasn't intended to be a quick hit and run—far from it. The intention was for much more of a long, patient game intended to position the company that would be called nChain and its wealth of patents in a commanding position in the world of blockchain.

Indeed, it was envisaged that the creation of such a comprehensive patent catalogue would take several years, and thereafter the vision was to create an engineering function to build proof of concept and also prototypes that could later be licensed as industry solutions. This patent catalogue and associated engineering vision was to be Craig Wright's sole focus. Others, as was his request to Matthews months earlier, would be managing the business side of things.

As soon as the Clayton Utz bill was settled, the law firm dropped Wright and DeMorgan as clients so as not to jeopardize any future disputes with the Australian Tax Office.

Meanwhile, Wright and his wife Ramona travelled to London in October 2015 and found a home to rent in Wimbledon as part of their employment contract with Tyche, while at the same time arranging that their furniture and belongings in Sydney could be packed up to be shipped overseas.

The deal of a lifetime was almost done, barring some final legal sign offs that would be undertaken in London in December 2015. Wright and his wealth of research into Bitcoin had been saved. The next phase of his life was about to begin.

"It wasn't so much the money," says Wright. "That part was just short term. The main thing was getting us out of that damn country and all the crap that went with it and setting us up somewhere else."

"Since probably the middle of 2013, I'd been observing what was happening in Bitcoin and I'd seen some worrying signs. Too many people were fixated with finding out who Satoshi really was," financial cryptographer Ian Grigg remembers.

Grigg—a fellow Australian—is a vitally important figure in the Bitcoin story. Grigg, again like Wright, had been a fringe figure in the cypherpunk movement dating back to the mid 1990s and had moved to Europe to explore concepts around digital cash and zero-coupon bonds while studying an MBA in London.

While lurking in the shadows of cypherpunk forums where one of the most prevalent conversations was the politics of finance on the internet, Grigg travelled to Amsterdam to work with his friend, Gary Howland, on an exchange-based project called Ricardo. As the story goes, Ricardo only came about at all because Grigg's own company, Systemics, had wanted to license software called eCash from DigiCash—one of the first attempts to put money onto the internet invented by the American computer scientist David Chaum in 1989. However, DigiCash wouldn't play ball.

"They wouldn't even talk to us," Grigg says. "And the reason they wouldn't," he explains, "is because David Chaum got carpeted by the Dutch National Bank for issuing what they thought was just toy money on the internet."

Grigg and Howland had to come up with their own design and then build it from scratch, both of which the two men did over a period of several months.

"It looked like a form of centralized Bitcoin, pseudonyms for control, but with a single server mediating all transactions," Grigg says. "We built it, and ran it, but I guess we were too early as we couldn't in those days find anyone who understood or believed. Or we didn't have the marketing chops to make our proposition presentable."

Grigg and Howland's business, as much as it was structurally sound, would ultimately prove to be too small to survive. Having burned through their capital in no time at all, they wound the Ricardo idea down. DigiCash as a broader concept failed too. Theoretically it worked, but in practice it didn't. The idea would ultimately be suffocated by a deal imposed upon them whereby they could only ever sell to banks. And in the year 2000, far too few banks were willing to come on-board to make it work.

"People forget that digital cash systems have been failing since the '80s," Craig Wright says. "And the reason it never got anywhere was because these guys were just anarchists. Chaum was an anarchist. These people kept trying to make a version of money that governments couldn't interact with."

For Ian Grigg however, his years spent working on Systemics and Ricardo concepts were not wasted time. As a result of his experimentation in the field, he was able to publish a number of highly influential papers covering relevant subjects such as triple-entry accounting. It is believed that some of the proposals outlined in Satoshi Nakamoto's white paper were inspired by elements of the writings of, among others, Ian Grigg.

Fast-forwarding to 2008, Grigg was still part of the cryptography community who first saw Satoshi Nakamoto's white paper when it was published.

"I maintained a watching brief on the cryptography mailing list," Grigg says. "When Satoshi released this white paper, like everyone else I read it, but I made a calculated decision not to participate in the conversations on the forum itself. The reason for my decision was that somebody else was on there with views that exactly reflected mine and he was diving into it so I just didn't need to."

Despite his interest in Satoshi's white paper from a broad cultural standpoint, Grigg didn't particularly think Bitcoin, the system that it described, could work in the real world of 2008. In simple terms, his main concern was that, by creating a situation whereby miners competed to inject more and more energy into a system, that system would only become more inefficient.

"As someone who'd spent my life trying to make systems efficient, I found Bitcoin's ethos to be a little offensive," Grigg says. "But with time I've had no choice but to accept it for what it is. That *was* the system. I still have my reservations however, even now. If you're going to use the amount of energy that Bitcoin requires and creates, you've got a responsibility to make best use of that energy. I wrote a paper about it all in 2011 called *Gresham's Law: The Inevitability of Collapse* which didn't exactly go down well."

Despite his protestations, in 2013 Grigg was still an avid observer of everything that was playing out in the world of Satoshi Nakamoto and by any measurement there was a lot happening. Like everyone else, he had seen how, after an initial flurry of engagement, Satoshi had retreated to who knows where, while handing control of the Bitcoin source code repository, network alert keys, and various web domains over to American computer scientist Gavin Andresen and others in the community. Satoshi Nakamoto's last email, to Bitcoin developer Mike Hearn in April of 2011, gave few clues as to future plans and instead read simply: "I have moved on to other things. It's in good hands with Gavin and everyone."

Grigg had also witnessed how, in the absence of their symbolic godhead figure, the Bitcoin community was steadily corrupting Satoshi's vision in a variety of attempts to make it fit their own purpose. Throughout 2013, he observed and schemed. By late 2014, because Grigg—a security specialist—started seeing some major red flags in the dog-eat-dog world of Bitcoin, he acted.

RELOCATION

"The question of Satoshi's identity was always getting bounced around. I'd seen the attempts to hack and extort and inevitably I too was getting asked this question, including in conversations with Adam Back at various times," recalls Grigg. "It got to the point where I actually found it all a bit distasteful and I thought grey-haired cryptography types like us should be focusing on other more important things like how Bitcoin could work. But people, including Adam, appeared to be fixated on finding out who Satoshi was."

Grigg's issue was that Back's actions were so wildly out of character. He and Back were both dyed-in-the wool members of the privacy community, where the concept of anonymity was sacrosanct.

"We weren't meant to be going out there doxxing people," Grigg says. "If anything, I thought we should be *protecting people*, rather than unravelling everything, especially someone with as much to offer the world as Satoshi. Eventually, Adam agreed with me, but then three days later he came back and said, 'Maybe it's this guy? What about that guy? What do you think?' I just threw my hands in the air in despair."

At that point, with names like Nick Szabo having been put forward, Grigg saw that there was a real problem that wasn't going to go away as long as Satoshi Nakamoto's true identity remained unknown. And that problem was that way too many people in the cryptography world were obsessed with trying to discover the truth.

"I thought to myself, *this is really interesting…*" says Grigg. "Here we had the privacy community who had now thrown away the mantle of privacy altogether and were trying to rip the anonymity from Satoshi Nakamoto. And I couldn't even convince Adam Back that this was happening."

Consequently, throughout late 2014, while observing endless chatter online, Grigg started formulating a plan to protect Satoshi Nakamoto.

"I basically did a traditional threat analysis, which was something we tended to do in the security industry," says Grigg. "You write them all down, number them all according to severity. And my conclusion was that Satoshi was afraid of something, was in danger, and needed protection."

Incredibly, Ian Grigg came to the conclusion that US government prosecutors represented the most severe threat to Satoshi Nakamoto. His argument centered upon the premise that US prosecutors, unlike their counterparts in other countries, often approached their role as a political position. To that extent, Grigg thought that it wasn't beyond the realms of possibility that, if Satoshi could be unmasked, one or more US prosecutors might view Satoshi as the ultimate trophy. Dragging Satoshi Nakamoto into court could well be a career-making move.

"These people are very good at constructing charges under which to drag people into court," says Grigg. "They usually go with the same two or three charges—'money laundering' is always in there—and they do this fully expecting two charges to get knocked out. As long as they have one charge that will stick however, they are in control."

Grigg started giving thought to the concept of putting Satoshi Nakamoto forward for the A.M. Turing Award, the computer science equivalent of a Nobel Prize, which is awarded to "an individual selected for contributions of a technical nature made to the computing community" and was first awarded in 1966. The thinking behind this was that Grigg's official recognition often acted as a deterrent to any potential prosecutors.

"It's more difficult to arrest someone when they have a high degree of standing in their particular field of expertise. An award only enhances that standing," Grigg says. With that, he began the lengthy process of creating an application to comprise supporting pieces written by prominent members of the computer science world.

CHAPTER **SEVEN**

Prometheus

Insulation from fame-hungry US prosecutors was just one of the fronts Ian Grigg was fighting on Satoshi Nakamoto's behalf. In parallel, other issues were brewing that were upping the stakes even further.

As much as anyone's anonymity is hard to preserve in today's internet world, Satoshi Nakamoto wasn't just anyone. Yes, Satoshi was an entity of huge influence and symbolism *because* their true identity was unknown. But equally, as much as Satoshi had, without a doubt, invented something revolutionary, not everyone in the community agreed about how that invention should be interpreted and deployed. People knew that they couldn't argue with a myth. But if that myth could be dismantled to reveal an actual person, maybe some influence could be exerted? Perhaps that's what Satoshi's pursuers were banking on.

Consequently, part of the responsibility for this desperate need to uncover Satoshi Nakamoto's identity could be attributed to divisions within the Bitcoin community itself. And one of the primary reasons for such tribalism was a historical and fundamental disaccord about how Bitcoin should scale (the number of transactions that can be completed per second) moving forward.

Ever since Satoshi Nakamoto had declared a 1MB block size limit in 2009, with no particular rationale to accompany it, it was obvious block size was always going to be a bone of contention in the world of Bitcoin. At the time, Satoshi, still so revered, simply stated that size limit would only be addressed in the future if there were ever to be a pressing need for it.

Within a year of that announcement however, some people in the Bitcoin community were already clamoring to increase the limit, which some argued was only ever intended to be a temporary measure in place to stop early Bitcoin miners performing what is called a DoS (Denial of Service) attack—where a blockchain network is 'attacked' and ultimately overwhelmed, usually by waves of malicious spam, with a view to impairing functionability.

Certain members of Bitcoin core development had other ideas. Some dug their heels somewhat by claiming that the block size limit was there for a specific reason—for example to stop the blockchain from becoming too big, or because small block size limits would encourage higher transaction fees and by extension would incentivize miners. This group became known as the "small-blockers." This was a highly divisive opinion, however.

This concept of limitation for many flew directly in the face of Satoshi Nakamoto's scaling vision for Bitcoin. In fact, the concept of block-size restraint completely *defeated the point* of the blockchain in the eyes of the other side of the debate, the "big-blocker" community, all of whom generally wanted the limit to increase so that the blockchain could scale, thus bringing transaction fees *down*. This era became known as the "The Scaling Debate."

Dialogue went back and forth during 2010 and early 2011 with Satoshi seemingly fending off opposing views as if the forums were a game of whack-a-mole. By and large, however, the message from the top remained consistent. In a direct response to Bitcoin core developer Jeff Garzik's suggestion in 2010 that the block size could be raised, Satoshi said that in 2010 the time just wasn't right, but that there was a possibility that a change could be hard-coded into the future to allow for an increase in block height in, say, 2011, thus giving users time to upgrade.

By 2013, greed and hunger for power had become the main a player in the Bitcoin story and it appeared that, with Satoshi long gone from the conversation, some saw this vacuum as an invitation to do with Bitcoin precisely as they wished. As it turned out, some took this as a cue not to honor Satoshi's incredible vision, but to forward their own selfish agendas. Meanwhile, vociferously tribal groups were springing up on sites like Reddit with strong opinions about the block size debate.

"Sometime in 2014 I had got on Skype with Adam Back and as we were talking, I got a sense that he was looking for a way to get some kind of commercial activity going in the Bitcoin space," Grigg recalls. "And then I said to him something along the lines of 'you and I—we're not really money men. We can't do the money because we don't know how to talk to the investors. We'd lose our integrity. What you need is a moneyman.' A month or so later, he told me he'd brought in Austin Hill and that was kind of the beginning of Blockstream."

Blockstream was essentially a rival "side chain" cofounded by Back—who Satoshi had name-checked in the white paper for his work on HashCash—engineer Greg Maxwell, and Belgian engineer Pieter Wullie.

"I always thought Blockstream was Greg's vision as our competition and that he chose Adam Back as a total puppet. Yes he had some street-cred because he was mentioned by Satoshi in the white paper and that of course goes a long way. But I don't think he's good at anything. Greg chose him because he could control him, in my opinion," says Kurt Wuckert Jr.

Founded in 2014 and launching in the latter part of 2015 with no obvious master plan other than to sweep up a bunch of Bitcoin developers and pay them a top-level salary, Blockstream seemed to exist to change bitcoin from being a scalable utility focused on electronic cash into being a straight-up store of value. Indeed, it would be hard to contest that Blockstream's function was little more than a thinly veiled Swiss bank for anyone lucky enough to be running on their software.

Crucially, the whole enterprise was funded by multiple rounds of underwriting from a cast of Silicone Valley heavyweight investors—thirty-one of them in in total. Even more significantly, all of Blockstream's investors each had ties to two very large entities within the financial industry: AXA Strategic Ventures, an entity that itself was linked to Bilderberg Group—an off-the-record conference that had met annually since 1954 with a vague remit to "foster relations between Europe and North America" and Digital Currency Group (DCG)—a group of venture capitalists founded by the well-known Wall Street investment banker Barry Silbert.

Gargantuan levels of backing aside, the bigger picture goal seemed to be that Blockstream was just the "respectable" front for a cynical small-blocker power play to seize control of the keys to Bitcoin kingdom, and to do so with big money behemoths lurking in the wings to supply the financial muscle when needed.

"People should pay more attention to Blockstream's name," Kurt Wuckert Jr. says, "What the fuck is a 'Blockstream'? It's a dam in the Bitcoin stream of possibility."

Ian Grigg, with no particular stake in the game of his own and as someone who maintained good relations with people on both sides of the block size debate, sat on the side-lines observing the Bitcoin world melting down in front of his eyes. While he could understand the motivations behind each side of the conversation, Grigg, an old-school guy who understood hardwired cypherpunk values like honor, integrity, and anonymity, saw something much more troubling out there in dog-eat-dog Bitcoin land.

"I came up with this thought experiment," Grigg says. "I'd seen many famous big innovations in the past. And if you look at the early history of those big innovations, they were generally one, two, or three people."

Grigg had grown up with the Unix (an earlier relative of the macOS) crowd and had attended the first university outside of the United States that taught it.

"I knew the whole backstory of Unix and it was fascinating to see how things happened. What struck me was that, in many cases, the inventors of these technologies got a really rough ride and did not get rewarded by society. Instead of getting any great monetary reward, they often ended up in scraps with financiers and ended up losing their shirts."

As much as Ian Grigg didn't particularly agree with Satoshi's design, he fully acknowledged the significance of what Satoshi had created. At the same time, he could also see a trend from the history of technological invention being repeated before his eyes.

"I started talking to older people in my circles—anyone who'd listen, basically—and many agreed with me. So, we formed an informal group—we called it the Prometheus Project—and the notion was to do whatever we could to give Satoshi a helping hand, protect Satoshi, and preserve the legend. This rolled along for a long while in some fashion. We created memes and we went out there, and at one point, we attacked people who were trying to doxx Satoshi using various Twitter gangs. I created the meme 'We Are All Satoshi' and our group spread it far and wide."

Central to Grigg's thinking was this suspicion that Satoshi Nakamoto was an informal team of individuals, rather than a lone figure.

"I'd figured it out by looking at how things were done," says Grigg. "There were certain questions that just couldn't be answered unless there was a team in place, for example, how all the communications were always so similar and perfect. Who does that? My view was that someone was writing the emails, then someone else was editing them. There was an editorial *process*. And so me and my little group of around six people started to spread this notion across the internet that Satoshi was a group assembled from several continents, and we did this to lessen the focus on Satoshi."

One of the people Grigg called upon to help him was a character by the name of Joseph Vaughn Perling (JVP, as he's known to the cryptography community). Vaughn Perling was a security and forensics expert with a dizzying area of experience spanning three decades. However, there was a reason Grigg drafted Vaughn Perling into Project Prometheus.

If Grigg is an important part of the Bitcoin story, JVP must deserve equal billing. Vaughn Perling, a mysterious character by anyone's standards, had been in the background of Bitcoin since the beginning in early 2009. However, early adoption wasn't JVP's only claim to fame. He had another that was far more impressive.

Joseph Vaughn Perling was one of the first people to come out and say publicly that he had met Satoshi Nakamoto, apparently at a hacker convention in Amsterdam called *What The Hack* in 2005, three years before Satoshi's white paper was published. Not only had he talked about the encounter to anyone who'd listen ever since, but he'd also written about the meeting in considerable depth in an article that would ultimately appear online.

In the article, Vaughn Perling describes an intelligent, quietly spoken, dark-haired man who was wary of keeping his personal space when talking. The two conversed for a while before the man launched into an earnest description not just of blockchain, but also of hashing algorithms and proof of work, all of which would later be found in Satoshi Nakamoto's white paper.

"By this time I'd realized that I wasn't talking to a random kook but a genius, and one who had thought this through in some great detail, and that this was pretty seriously interesting stuff. What he was working on was truly amazingly revolutionary and I started to get a bit animated, and excited. I asked him if he realized how incredible this was and the impact it would have on the world. I was very much excited at this point. He kept his demeanor more calm than mine but there was a bit of a smile on his face and a twinkle in his eye as he could see the effect he was having on me as the implications were becoming more and more clear," Vaughn Perling's article said.

Whoever Vaughn Perling was talking to in 2005 was offering a verbal prophecy of something that would later come to be. After more explanation, the two men discussed working together when the time came to start writing the code for the mysterious man's incredible idea. Ultimately, Vaughn Perling politely passed on the offer suggesting that others from within the cypherpunk community might be better suited to the task. However, as the two men wound up their talk, the man told Vaughn Perling to look out for his invention down the line. When Vaughn Perling asked what the name of the secret project would be, the man paused.

"This seemed to trigger a thought in his head, which appeared to me as a trust evaluation and though was clear to me that he had a project name in mind, but that he was reluctant to say it. The man was clearly good at keeping secret things secret and I respected that quite a lot," Vaughn Perling's article further says.

Before Vaughn Perling let his new acquaintance disappear into the crowded throng of the convention, perhaps never to be seen or heard from again, he asked him one more question.

"So I asked him how I would know his project from other similar efforts, and that is when he told me to look for him, Satoshi Naka-

moto. I had never heard this before (and indeed perhaps no one had in 2005) and it seemed not to match at all with the person to whom I was speaking so I asked him to repeat it, which he did—Satoshi Nakamoto."

Clearly, on July 29th, 2005, Joseph Vaughn Perling had met the inventor of Bitcoin. Nobody else could possibly have known what the man knew. Nobody else could have possibly described so succinctly and accurately the contents of a white paper that would not exist for another three years. His meeting with the man who called himself Satoshi Nakamoto in 2005 is by far the most plausible account in existence of a random encounter with the person who invented Bitcoin.

"I don't actually remember him," Wright says. "He seems to have a photo of me which I don't remember anyone taking it but I went to so many of these conferences I wouldn't have a clue. He remembers much more than I do."

In 2015, Ian Grigg and Joseph Vaughn Perling worked together on the final version of Vaughn Perling's article with the intention to publish it wherever and however they could. In the end it was passed to a third party who leaked it online on their behalf, initially in 2015. It was later updated in 2016 to include Wright's name.

"I was working with JVP in early 2015 to edit and improve the document. At first he held Craig's name and person out of it. But as we moved forward, he admitted it was Craig he had met," says Grigg. "Given all the times we discussed it and the versions the document went through, there's little doubt in the big picture story that the two of them met at the Dutch tech event. If I have a doubt it is whether Craig described the whole of Bitcoin so completely. In 2005 I don't think he had a completed design in his head. In concept, yes, but it still had to be built, and generally things morph a little in the building as unplanned impacts are discovered," he continues.

Meanwhile, having helped Vaughn Perling with his article in early 2015, Ian Grigg was unwittingly forging another key relationship online as part of his Project Prometheus plans.

"Somebody replied to me on Twitter about something, as often happens," Grigg recalls. "I believe they were aware of what I was trying to do with the Prometheus stuff and they sent me a direct message just to say hello. From there I started interacting with this person cautiously and two things became apparent to me. One, this person knew far too much about Bitcoin to not be involved in some way, and two, this person seemed to be very intelligent, but also under a lot of personal stress of some kind. Quite wild, actually."

Although he didn't know it at first, Ian Grigg was conversing with another enigmatic and highly significant player in the Bitcoin story, Uyen T. Nguyen—known in some circles as, "The Intern" and in others as "The Director."

"I established that Uyen had found Craig the same way she had found me. Basically, she had a habit of running around the internet looking for interesting people to talk to. Initially, she talked mostly to Dave Kleiman because she had bought and read a security book that Dave and Craig had written in 2008 while she was still in Vietnam entitled *Overwriting Hard Drive Data: The Great Wiping Controversy*. Apparently, she had made money in Vietnam by buying up textbooks and selling them to other students. At the same time, she was reading and absorbing all these books," Ian Grigg says.

Little is known about Nguyen other than she's of Vietnamese descent and was born in 1992. Beyond that, it gets vague other than she was reputedly an IT specialist and math prodigy who transferred from Vietnam to a US university to study on a scholarship.

"Uyen, who will now be in her twenties, was like a puppy when I first met her. I'm not trying to sound mean, that's just how she was," Wright explains. "She found me because of all my strands for patents sometime in 2010 or 2011. By that point I had seventeen or eighteen different qualifications in information security and was already more qualified than anyone else on earth and she basically started stalking me, mostly on social media, because of that," he adds.

Somehow, not long after reaching the US, she managed to persuade Dave Kleiman to take her on as an intern so that he could teach her the business side of what he and Wright were doing related to Bitcoin. What she was actually doing is a little hazy. What is less hazy is that Nguyen reputedly had a highly volatile personality.

By the middle of 2011, by which time Satoshi Nakamoto had stepped away from the Bitcoin community, Wright and Kleiman continued to work on Bitcoin-related projects with Nguyen learning the Bitcoin ropes in the background. Meanwhile, presumably to insulate his and Kleiman's bitcoin mining proceeds from the grasping tentacles of the ATO, Wright created the first Tulip Trust, whereupon Kleiman was asked to sign an agreement that stated that he would hold the now infamous 1,100.111 bitcoins, which, at the time, was worth just £100,000. Some of the coins went into a trust in Seychelles, the others into another in Singapore. Not long after The Tulip Trust was said to have been set up, Nguyen was fast-tracked, for reasons that aren't immediately clear, to a disproportionately elevated role for someone so young and inexperienced within Wright and Kleiman's company, W&K Info Defense LLC (W&K), and from there she only became more powerful. Some even claimed that Nguyen was at one point appointed to stand as a trustee.

"This is what people get wrong," Wright says. "Uyen was never a member of the trust. I held multiple things and she was just entrusted with holding some key slices (keys for a multi-signature Bitcoin wallet, broken down into slices and distributed widely for added security) at one stage. She was never 'a trustee.' She often exaggerated what she could do, but Dave liked and trusted her."

Whatever it was that Uyen Nguyen actually did day-to-day. and for whatever reason she was entrusted with so much authority within Craig Wright's world, didn't matter. Uyen Nguyen, herself operating from the shadows of the internet, had become Wright's trusted gatekeeper.

"In hindsight, I probably gave Uyen more responsibility than she was ready for," Wright says. "But she kept wanting to do things so I just let her."

By early 2015 when she ran into Ian Grigg on Twitter while she was co-managing the account entitled "Tulip Boy," she was clearly well-versed in every aspect of Wright's business, especially, it seems, regarding the details of both his issues with the tax office, and the sustained nature of the hacking attempts he was being subjected to.

"I'd been talking to this person for a while and there came a point that, although she didn't initially admit it, I realized she was part of the informal Satoshi 'team' idea that I had already guessed existed. In fact, by that time, I think there were just two team members left: Satoshi and the person I was talking to," Ian Grigg says.

It would be some time before Uyen would reveal to Grigg that she was in fact a member of the informal team Satoshi, however. But when she did, a couple of months after the first contact, whether she intended to or not, she began feeding Grigg a startling insight into Wright's inner world.

"Uyen's stories weren't always totally accurate," Grigg says. "There were certain aspects she emphasized or even over emphasized, and there were certain other things she failed to spot at all. But, I was presented with background information on what had been happening. I was told that some of Craig's employees had indeed been trying to steal Craig's IP since as far back as 2007.

Craig had put together a team, and he used that team to build software. Some of the people working for him decided that they wanted to hack him to steal code from him with a view to collapsing the company and going off and using the IP," Grigg says.

It appears that, while this lengthy conspiracy to steal Wright's IP might not have been totally successful; there was a lot of damage done to the business in the process. Whether *this* was the reason why Craig Wright's company DeMorgan was in a state of such disarray, is unclear. But in combination with the financial issues caused by Wright's rejected Research and Development claims, it's easy to see how things had come such to an unpleasant head by 2015.

"To what extent Craig was also shooting himself in the foot with dodgy claims that Bitcoin was an innovation and therefore the Australian government should pay him for R&D, I'm not sure. Craig seemed very miffed about all that, but to the rest of us it was obvious that the Australian government weren't going to go along with it," Grigg says.

The information being presented to Grigg through his conversations with Nguyen paint a clear picture and point to a blend of issues that left Wright in a position where he'd simply run out of business moves to make.

"If you're not a particularly good CEO or manager of companies, you start making crazy decisions under pressure," says Grigg. "And crazy things come to find you. Craig certainly seemed to have made a mess of things."

Eventually, having demonstrated over many months that he was a trustworthy and sympathetic ear for the highly-strung Uyen Nguyen's concerns, it was suggested that Wright and Grigg could meet in person.

"He was badgered by the intern to meet up with me," Grigg told *CoinGeek* in 2021. "I think she had the view that I should be employed by the organization, that I should become part of the bigger picture of what would later become nChain. I just wanted to find out. I wanted to confirm my hypothesis that this was Satoshi," he continued.

"You've got to meet Craig," Uyen told Grigg. "He's a good guy."

"Sure," Grigg said. "When is he next in London?"

In the process of setting up his move to begin working with the soon-to-be created new business, Wright was in London on several occasions after the initial deal was signed in Sydney on June 29. During one trip, he and fellow Australian Ian Grigg found themselves together in a London pub—The Duke of York on Dering Street—enjoying a few beers and a burger.

"I don't need a second invitation to go to a pub," says Grigg "That's what we Australians do. If I remember the evening correctly, Craig actually got a bit merry."

Social aspirations aside, Grigg approached the meeting with Wright strategically, and specifically with a view to establishing whether the man he would spend three hours drinking beer with in a London pub was in fact the inventor of Bitcoin.

"I went in there with a few test questions in my mind—not that it would have been obvious to him that they were test questions," Grigg says. "Although I had more or less got the information out of Uyen by this point, when I met Craig, we were still playing this kind of game. I don't know if he had considered whether I knew he was Satoshi or not, but I was going in there fairly convinced that this guy was the leader of the team. I just wanted to prove it to myself."

To establish Wright's connection to Satoshi Nakamoto, Grigg constructed tests, all of which Craig Wright passed with flying colors.

"One of them was related to his technical knowledge," Grigg told *CoinGeek*. "He came up with some particular construct and I said, 'No, that's not true. That can't be true. There's no way that can be done.'"

Grigg and Wright had been discussing an aspect of the most recent internet protocol IPv6 as far as how it related to Bitcoin. Wright told Grigg that the size of the IPv6 number was the same size as a Bitcoin key. What that meant was that they could be constructed to be the same. And if you could construct them to be the same, two people with IPv6 numbers could do elliptic curve cryptography directly with each other without any fee exchange.

"That would have been huge," says Grigg. "And the reason I said that it couldn't be done was because I knew that the intelligence agencies were all through the groups that create the technical standards that drove the internet. They were in there making sure certain things didn't happen—and what Craig was describing to me was one of those things. It would have blown their minds. They'd have been all over it. But Craig said, 'No. Go and have a look at this RFC (Request For Comment).' When I got home that night, I dragged out the RFC and had a look at it and sure enough, he was right. I was flabbergasted. It was interesting to me because people had talked about IPv6 for twenty years. And nobody had ever mentioned what Craig told me. For something like that to have snuck in and for him to know about it, was very revealing."

Grigg's second test was pitched to Wright just before the two were leaving the pub for the evening.

"I've got a bunch of mates," Grigg began, "and we spend a lot of time thinking about Satoshi. Between us we try to think of ways to steer the industry to make things easier for Satoshi, to stop the attacks and the attempts to doxx," he continued.

Grigg also explained that he'd started the lengthy process of assembling supporting documents and papers for the forthcoming A.M. Turing Award application.

"I need people to help write for me—'the case for Satoshi,'" Grigg told Wright. "Can you help me?"

Without a pause, Wright replied.

"No. I can't help you."

"His response was so immediate and so definitive," Grigg says. "Anyone else would have said, 'Oh really? How interesting. Let me think about it.' But he didn't. He just shut it down. And in doing so he was revealing himself as Satoshi. He couldn't help me because he *was* Satoshi."

Apparently, Wright himself was a little startled by his own response to Grigg's question to the extent that he half-heartedly tried to explain why is 'No' response had been so firm.

"I was playing a game," Grigg admits. "And I was being a bit Machiavellian about it all. Whether he realized this at the time, I'm not sure."

Not long after The Duke of York pub meeting, in further conversations with Uyen Nguyen, it was definitely relayed to Grigg that Craig Wright was indeed Satoshi Nakamoto, the creator of Bitcoin.

"It was an informal conversation, but at the same time it was information that she assumed I would keep to myself," Grigg explains.

Grigg and Wright would meet on a couple of subsequent occasions during 2015, with Wright gradually parting with valuable nuggets of information about the technical aspects of his work dating back many years.

"I found myself having to be patient and to allow Craig to drive the conversations," Grigg remembers. "I'd throw in a few questions from time to time—many of them weren't answered."

But some *were* answered, including some fascinating details regarding some of the intricacies of the origins of the Bitcoin code.

"I got the impression that Craig's grandfather was an extremely important part of the story," Grigg says. "Not only that, I found out that somehow the grandfather knew David Rees, one of Britain's foremost mathematicians, who worked at Bletchley Park during World War II."

Born in Abergavenny, Wales in 1918, Rees had a decorated academic career in mathematics before being drafted in to work at Hut 6 of Bletchley Park in late 1939. Situated on Bletchley Estate near Milton Keynes, Bletchley Park was a large country house that housed the Government Code and Cipher School (GC & CS), which specialized in penetrating the codes of the Axis Powers—especially the German Enigma and Lorenz codes. According to historical experts, Bletchley "Ultra" intelligence shortened the war significantly and one of the main players in the group of code-breakers was Alan Turing.

"I was told that Craig's grandfather knew David Rees from back in their earlier years and introduced him at some point many years later to Craig. David Rees became a mentor and responded to emails for a long period of time," says Grigg

While Wright had many skills, cryptography was never his strongest suit in the years immediately before 2008. Because of his connection to David Rees, he was able to learn what he needed to make Bitcoin work as it did.

"Craig made a very interesting choice, which was not understandable given the times," Grigg explains. "He decided to use what is referred to as the K1 curve in his code, as opposed to the R1 curve as used by everyone else."

The question therefore was: why had Craig Wright used this obscure K1 curve in his design for Bitcoin? How did Craig Wright, a modest cryptographer at best, even know about the K1 curve?

"The R1 curve was created by NIST—the American standards organization—with an unknown set of parameters. This meant that the NSA were probably involved. Whereas K1 was created by taking the cubed root of sixty-four and then parceling up the various fractional numbers and putting them into the parameters. It was a known method, and therefore less likely to be interfered with by the NSA," Grigg continues.

In 2008, nobody particularly noticed the K1 curve in Bitcoin, but Craig Wright had definite reasons for putting it there.

"His mentor was a cryptographer of long and deep standing, including operating with the UK government on top secret projects for many years. It is my view that Craig was advised to use R1 by David Rees," Ian Grigg says.

Grigg's pub conversations with Wright in 2015 had therefore cast even more light on the concept of Wright being the man behind the white paper, and by extension, the inventor of Bitcoin, but with vital assistance from other people along the way. Ian Grigg's view (and he'd later be proved correct) was that David Rees was a key member of the Satoshi team. Without his cryptography input, Bitcoin wouldn't have been the revolutionary creation that it was and is.

CHAPTER **EIGHT**

Unmasked

By late summer of 2015, as much as Ian Grigg knew that Craig Wright was Satoshi Nakamoto, many other people also did. The chatter had reached a fever pitch and the secret was inevitably going to come out. For Craig Wright, real trouble was brewing.

"It was feeding back to us that a lot of people knew—some very adversarial people at that," says Grigg. "The magazine journalists who would later out Craig Wright had started getting their sources from this ever-widening circle of people. I don't think it was such a big deal that I found out when I did. I could see the whole thing was about to come unstuck."

Meanwhile Wright met Nguyen in person for the first and only time. For some time, Wright had been paying for Nguyen to attend SANS (SysAdmin, Audit, Network, and Security) training courses as part of her compensation for being employed and the two ended up at the same event in September of 2015 in Las Vegas, by which time the young intern apparently had romantic notions about her boss.

"By this time, Uyen was getting quite hysterical," Wright says. "She ended up camping outside my hotel room waiting for me to come out. I was married. I had no interest at all."

"At the end of that week, Uyen flew home to L.A., was picked up by an uncle, driven back to LAX, and flew to meet me in New York to do a small security review for a company that did suicide SMS response," Ian Grigg recalls. "Boy did I get an earful about Craig. To me it looked as if it was very hard for her to focus on the job at hand."

Las Vegas—October 29, 2015

Craig Wright's face, a little fuzzy or pixelated, beamed onto a video screen at a Bitcoin Investor Conference.

The event was being compèred by a female hostess who went by the name of Michele Seven—a self-confessed Libertarian who'd resisted filing a federal tax return in 2007 and was hit with a $640,000 tax bill as a result. Additionally, as an unashamed advocate of underground marketplaces, Michele Seven, who also went by the pseudonym "BitcoinBelle" online and was known for her activism around the trial of Ross Ulbricht, the alleged founder of Silk Road.

Wright was in London, on one of a few trips he made with his wife Ramona, to prepare for his permanent move prior to taking up his new role as Chief Science Officer at nChain. Also on the panel that day was something of an all-star cast of personalities from the tech world that included computer scientist Nick Szabo, former government official Edmund Moy, Joseph Vaughn Perling, and Trace Mayer, an entrepreneur and monetary scientist.

It all began quite normally. The hostess welcomed Wright and he began by talking for a few seconds about what he did.

"Okay," Wright began, "first of all, I'm a former academic who, these days, does research commercially that nobody ever hears about, which suits me very well." He continued, "I basically work in designing protocols and doing a whole lot of things that people don't realize is actually possible yet."

Then he paused. It was quite a long pause. "Well…" Wright began again, "I'll be back to publishing papers again soon. I haven't been for a while. It has been a few years now. I'll be going back to that next year…"

At that moment, as Wright was seemingly building quite a head of steam, Michelle Seven did something quite unexpected. She pulled the rug.

"But hold on a minute," she said, while Wright was still talking. "Who are you? What are you? Tell me who you are? Are you a computer scientist? Are you a miner?" she asked.

"I'm a bit of everything," Wright interjected. "I have a master's in Law from over here in Northumbria, in England. I have a master's in statistics, a couple of doctorates…I forget actually what I've got these days," he said, staring directly into the camera and smiling mischievously.

"That's a lot of certificates," Seven said, laughing a little too nervously for anyone's comfort. An awkward silence followed.

"How did you first learn about Bitcoin?" she asked next. Wright paused and his eyes looked up and to his left before he responded as if he was summoning inspiration from a parallel universe.

"Umm, I've been involved in all this for a long time," he replied. "I try and stay…I keep me head down…"

"Were you a miner?" Seven repeated.

Wright paused again. "A long time ago," he eventually said with an expression that might as well have been accompanied by an exaggerated wink.

From that point the panel discussion delved into the intricacies of Bitcoin and a now famous argument between Wright and Szabo, a man who ironically some had previously believed might be Satoshi, about whether Bitcoin was "Turing Complete" (able to solve any computational problem, basically).

"Nick Szabo didn't invent smart contracts and didn't do half the things people claim," Wright says. "He's got a bachelor's degree and wrote a few blogs about other people's work and that's it."

As much as Wright publicly sparring with Szabo grabbed people's attention at the time, it was Wright's introductory sequence that was perhaps most revealing. Maybe a secret had almost slipped out.

On reflection, Wright's body language and responses were every bit as bizarre as Michele Seven's demeanor and angle of questioning—to the extent that it almost looked as if Wright was subtly, but publicly, confessing to the world for the first time that he was Satoshi Nakamoto, the inventor of Bitcoin who hadn't been heard from since March 2014 when posting the words "I am not Dorian Nakamoto" on the PSP Foundation forum. This had been in response to a major news story that had broken claiming that Bitcoin's inventor was a Japanese American man living in California—even though the man himself denied any connection to the alias and said he knew nothing about Bitcoin.

But Wright didn't confess, not quite—even though toward the end of the event he again strayed close to an admission when stating: "If I don't want to go out there and say, 'I'm a billionaire,' or 'I'm running X, Y or Z'—I shouldn't have to tell people that."

At the same time, it appeared as if Seven might have realized who exactly was in her midst and found herself, subconsciously or otherwise, backtracking and asking Wright to identify himself even though Wright told me himself that it was she who had invited him to appear in the first place and presumably she knew exactly who he was and what he did.

There was, however, an explanation. Michele Seven knew *exactly* who Craig Wright was in October 2015. And the reason she did was because the two had met on Twitter a few months prior and there had been intermittent back and forth about Bitcoin and whatever else.

"I had met Michele Seven on Twitter at the beginning of 2015," says Wright. "We had a bit of an ongoing conversation. I didn't tell her explicitly that I was Satoshi but I know that someone else had. Much later, I found out that she was in some way involved in me being outed. I believe she was in contact with both publications and, possibly, Ira Kleiman and others."

It is perhaps no surprise either that JVP—who, since meeting Craig Wright in 2005, had founded New Liberty Dollar in 2013 (a private currency which he described simply as a "silver piece medallion") would also appear on a Las Vegas panel of experts where one of the guests was the man he had met ten years previously and who'd told him about his vision, Bitcoin. So while Michele Seven seemed to know who and what Wright was from her dialogue directly with him on Twitter, Joseph Vaughn Perling also did.

Was all this just a coincidence? Probably not...

The Las Vegas conference of October 2015 appears to have been a carefully arranged set-up, specifically tailored to encourage Craig Wright to reveal himself as Satoshi Nakamoto, presumably before somebody else did it for him—and for some of the foremost people in the industry like Nick Szabo to be right there in the room to see it all happen. For whatever reason, Wright didn't take the bait that Seven so wanted him to take.

"Michele Seven thought I was Satoshi but when she met me I wasn't the kind of Satoshi she'd been hoping for," Wright explains. "I think she assumed I was some kind of anarchist and wanted me to help her brother who was in prison, wanted me to help with Ross Ulbricht—neither of which I was ever going to do. Seven was just a troublemaker, really."

While the bizarre interaction on October 29th, 2015 might not have registered with anyone who witnessed it in real time, the events of the next month or so would focus considerable retrospective attention on Wright's appearance in Las Vegas for anyone who cared to connect the dots—dots that had been coalescing for some time.

December 8, 2015

The pressure on Craig Wright was ramping up. One of the two publications that would ultimately out him was contacting Wright directly and saying something to the effect of, "we've got information that has been provided to us that indicates to us that you are Satoshi Nakamoto. We have done our research, we've dug into this, and authenticated documents. We believe that you are Satoshi and we are going to publish a story to that effect and we want you to comment before we do so."

"One of the journalists even contacted me to see what I knew," Ian Grigg recalls. "But I didn't reply."

"When I was helping Craig organize his affairs in Sydney in December, he started receiving messages," Stefan Matthews recalls. "He was literally sitting a meter away from me in his office when these messages came in over a couple of days and I could tell that he was getting more and more agitated about the possibility that someone was going to go public with a story pointing at him."

Wright was in an impossible position—truly between a rock and a hard place. And the pressure wasn't letting up one bit.

Seemingly, whoever contacted him, as if to reinforce their seriousness, also gave him a flavor of what they had.

"They wanted me to confirm I was Satoshi," Wright says. I replied and said basically that they shouldn't have what they've got and asked how the hell they had got it."

Stefan Matthews kicked into damage limitation mode by sending Robert MacGregor in Vancouver copies of the communications between Wright and the journalist. MacGregor may have deliberated—who knows—but he didn't blink.

"His response to me was 'Tell Craig to do nothing. Tell him not to reply further. There is no way a publication is going to go out with a story of this magnitude without having spoken to Craig to get his side of the story,'" Stefan Matthews recalls.

"I thought there was more we could do—maybe injunct them or something, but we didn't do anything," Wright says

A line in the sand was being drawn. And if ever there was something that symbolized the beginning of a division between Craig Wright and Rob MacGregor—one of the people responsible for brokering the most significant deal of Wright's life—it was this line.

"Craig was distraught," Matthews says. "He was sitting there saying, 'I can't just sit here and do nothing.' Meanwhile, I was trying to reassure him by saying 'Rob's supposedly got experience in this area and he's saying there's no fucking way in the world they'll release this story without your comment.'"

But Robert Macgregor was wrong.

A little over a month after almost revealing his identity at the conference in Las Vegas, Craig Steven Wright's public life changed forever on December 8th, 2015, when a *WIRED* article by Andy Greenberg and a *Gizmodo* article by Andy Cush and Sam Biddle went public with stories claiming that he, at the age of forty-five, was Satoshi Nakamoto, the inventor of Bitcoin.

Although the publications' pieces drew from the same trove of documents as evidence, each had a slightly different slant on the story.

"This Australian says he and his dead friend invented Bitcoin," the *Gizmodo* header said.

"Bitcoin's creator Satoshi Nakamoto is probably this unknown Australian," *WIRED's* went with.

"I was not surprised that he was Satoshi, it was now public what I had thought for a long time," Lynn Wright says.

"I knew he was Satoshi," John Chesher says.

"The unmasking was a complete surprise to me," says Stephanae Savanah. "But having said that, a few weeks—*or months?*—previously, Craig had attended a Bitcoin conference online, which I later saw on YouTube. He spoke authoritatively about Bitcoin technology and its potential for innovative applications across all industries. I cannot remember the name of the conference or other details such as date /location. However, I do remember an attendee directly asking Craig if he was Satoshi Nakamoto. Craig did not admit he was Satoshi Nakamoto but this may have been the first inkling in the Bitcoin world that he is Satoshi."

"I was back in the office in Sydney when the articles came out," Wright recalls. "My first thought was *Fuck*. I did occasionally think that my identity might come out one day but I didn't think it would be like that."

For the news outlets themselves, many months of detailed investigative work were finally over. They had delivered their man to the world on a silver platter, they must have thought.

For the wider tech world, there was a payoff too in the sense that seven years of debate, chatter, and speculation had not been for nothing. Instead, *WIRED* and *Gizmodo* had dovetailed their investigative work to provide what on the surface looked like the immaculate reveal. Best of all perhaps, instead of merely chasing ghosts forever—and there had been many to chase—in the unlikely guise of Craig Steven Wright, Bitcoin devotees finally had a tangible flesh and blood figurehead who existed in the real world. Whether he was actually their messiah wasn't important on December 8th of 2015. At least he was real.

For Craig Wright, there was no upside whatsoever. The publications' revelations, the majority of them of a negative slant, were just the beginning of a nightmare that he must have known would one day come ever since the moment he bequeathed his Bitcoin white paper to the world seven years previously.

"Before all this I was a very private person. I'd done a couple of expert interviews for the BBC that nobody ever cared about. But this was ridiculous," says Wright.

Had he really thought it possible to remain masked by a pseudonym for the rest of his life—especially in the internet age where everything and everyone is findable one way or another? As a forensic computer scientist himself, he must have known that by attempting to live a parallel life he was only playing a long game of cat and mouse that he could only lose.

"The whole thing was vindictive and some of the people involved, Andy Cush for example, were ultra-anarchist types and I was the exact opposite," Wright says. "I suppose I just hoped I could continue with my life and keep coding, but when it happened I realized that by outing me, these people played into the hands of my enemies. Now people knew who I hated and who hated me."

Regardless, the big reveal happened very much against his will, and it wasn't as if Wright hadn't been given ample warning in advance.

As the story goes, the publications had been receiving this information from an anonymous source close to Wright who then began leaking it to a pseudonymous internet security researcher familiar with darknet markets and Bitcoin named Gwern Branwen. Branwen then made the documents available to one or both of the publications.

"I hacked Satoshi Naklamoto (sic)," the initial message said. "These files are all from his business account. The person is Dr. Craig Wright."

"At the time, I suspected my intern Uyen was the source who leaked the information. Me being like I am I just asked her straight out, 'Have you done this?' and of course she got really upset and told me to fuck off, but it wasn't her," says Wright. "Then I thought it was one of my former Hotwire staff members whose laptop had a copy of my wife Ramona's private emails on it but at the time I couldn't prove anything."

Without comment from Wright, both *WIRED* and *Gizmodo* produced documents that their sources had acquired ranging from blog posts, emails between Craig Wright and Dave Kleiman in 2008 where they discussed the idea of Kleiman editing a white paper about Bitcoin prior to the paper's release in October of that year.

In another later email to Kleiman in September of 2011, Wright wrote, "I cannot do the Satoshi bit anymore. They no longer listen. I am better as a myth."

Other email exchanges between Craig Wright, his lawyer Andrew Sommer, and the Australian Tax Office and minutes of meetings that Wright, John Chesher, and Andrew Sommer had with tax office officials were also released. The latter suggested that the officials had been aware that Wright was the man behind the Nakamoto alias all along.

Perhaps the most compelling piece of evidence of all however was an email exchange from the hacked account where a message dated January 8th, 2014 showed Wright emailing his wife, Andrew Sommer, and John Chesher from satoshi@vistomail.com, the email address that Satoshi used throughout 2009 and 2010 to email early Bitcoin developers and users.

In this particular email exchange, which carried the subject line, "Fear of The Future," Wright suggests approaching an Australian Senator, Arthur Sinodinos, as part of his increasingly desperate attempts to get some closure on how Bitcoin should be regulated.

"Hello Andrew," the email began. "How do we get the good senator involved? Would our Japanese friend have weight coming out of retirement or not?" The email was then signed "Craig (possibly...)."

Wright was explicitly asking if unmasking himself as being Satoshi would carry influence with a Government official.

The *WIRED* and *Gizmodo* articles not only made for fascinating reading given the prurient nature of the access to Wright's private communications, but they also seemed to offer the most definitive case ever put forward regarding the true identity of Satoshi Nakamoto. For a while, it genuinely seemed as if one of the internet's greatest ever myths had been busted. Even Wright's most ardent critics would surely find the weight of evidence produced to be too much to refute.

"The articles going to press set off a whole chain of things," Stefan Matthews recalls. "When the stories went out, the Federal Police raided Craig's home and his offices on the same day."

Matthews was sitting in the business class lounge at Sydney airport awaiting a flight to Manila on the morning the articles dropped. As Matthews was awaiting the call to board his flight, Wright's DeMorgan colleague Allan Pedersen called him and told him the alarming news. A few minutes later, he received a second call from Pedersen to say that that federal police were swarming all over DeMorgan's office out in North Ryde.

The warrant, he was told, had been issued by the Australian Tax Office under the Australian Crimes Act 1914 and they were to look for "originals or copies" of material held on computer hard drives, photographs, and bank statements—basically anything they could lay their hands on. Also on the warrant was a list of companies and individuals. One of the names on the list was Satoshi Nakamoto.

"Apparently, they wanted to establish once and for all whether DeMorgan's research office was just the front for a fraud where Wright was claiming R&D rebates for research that didn't exist," says Matthews.

Panicking, Matthews requested that his luggage be removed from his forthcoming flight at the last minute. This was a demand that prompted an even more panicked reaction from airline staff that perhaps feared that Matthews might have had a bomb in his luggage or something equally alarming.

Matthews was taken into the bowels of Sydney Airport and quizzed at length by security staff about his sudden actions. When they realized there was no danger, he was released to go back through customs and immigration in reverse before reclaiming the rental car he'd dropped off two hours earlier.

While driving, Matthews received a call from John Balazs—a partner in the law firm Balazs, Lazanas, and Welch who'd been retained on tax matters. Balazs explained that he was doing what he could to get to the bottom of what was a fast-evolving situation.

"All I knew was that it wasn't a criminal probe per se," Matthew says. "The ATO had simply asked federal police to seize digital records."

When Matthews arrived at DeMorgan's office in North Ryde he was confronted by a chaotic scene outside it. Rumors had been circulating in the media for some time and the *WIRED* and *Gizmodo* articles had pushed interest over the edge to the point of near hysteria. Consequently, press were milling around; cameras were everywhere. The building itself was also crawling with people in uniform—federal police—who initially prevented Matthews from entering. Once he had persuaded them who he was and why he was there, Matthews walked inside the DeMorgan office to be met by a scene that resembled a swarm of locusts, with police officers thrusting USB sticks into every computer in an attempt to suck out whatever information remained.

"Not only were they removing information from the machines," Matthews says, "but someone from Craig's team had given the cops all the access passwords and this allowed them to remove data from cloud storage."

"Just tell us what it is that you need," Matthews said to one of ranking officers. "There is no compromising information being hidden here whatsoever. So, please just tell us what you're looking for and this can all be done much more quickly."

After a couple of hours, the same ranking officer informed Matthews that they also had a warrant to search Wright's house at 43 St. Johns Avenue in the Gordon district north of the city and demanded the name of the rental agent so they could get keys, otherwise they'd be forced to break down the doors to gain access.

Wright however, was long gone. He and his wife Ramona had vacated the house several weeks previously and their furniture and belongings had long since been shipped to the UK. Indeed, Wright's wife had been living in London since late August. Since early September, Wright's son had already been enrolled at and had been attending ASL—The American School—in London. Wright himself had been in London pretty much full-time since October.

The Wrights' whole *life* was in London. However, while loose ends relating to DeMorgan's IP were still being tied up, Wright and his wife frequently travelled back and forth to Australia. On this particular trip in December they'd been staying in a luxury apartment in Meriton World Tower in a different part of Sydney, all arranged by Stefan Matthews.

Nevertheless, Matthews obtained the keys to 43 St. Johns Avenue from one of the girls in the DeMorgan office who was arranging for the house to be cleaned. The officials then went to the property, which by this time was also thronged with reporters who'd been alerted to the bizarre story that was unfolding.

Several hours later, after an exhaustive but fruitless search, the federal officers emerged from the Wright's former home with nothing of consequence. There were no documents, no laptops full of incriminating evidence; the rack of computers that had apparently been fed by a room of heavy-duty generators at the rear of the property, were long gone.

"Computers become obsolete very quickly," Wright says. "Stefan eventually sold all my stuff for scrap."

After the officials came up with nothing, Matthews resisted the urge to say something to the effect of, "I told you so."

Meanwhile, he had bigger problems. Another more pressing situation was developing twenty-four miles to the South in central Sydney.

"While the officials were turning Craig's house upside down, Craig called me to say that there was a problem in the city," Matthews recalls.

Someone had given the police the address of where Wright and his wife Ramona were staying at the Meriton Towers. Seemingly, the police had shown up at the front desk and were demanding entrance to Wright's suite, which was on the sixty-third floor.

The desk staff buzzed up to Wright's suite on the intercom and his wife Ramona answered. They were told that the police were on their way up. Wright and Ramona looked at each other. They had little time to deliberate. In the space of a couple of hours, police had swooped on their office and their former home and here they now were at their temporary apartment suite. It felt as if they had run out of moves to make. At that moment, the two agreed that Wright should leave and Ramona would stay to talk to the police when they arrived.

Wright, meanwhile, still dressed in shorts and a t-shirt, grabbed a large laptop computer and a cell phone belonging to Ramona. Assuming that the police would be coming up in the elevator, he scrambled down the stairs to the sixty-first floor where there was a leisure suite with a swimming pool and some offices.

Ramona Wright waited for the police to arrive—which they duly did after a few minutes. Realizing that Wright had gone and there was nothing to find in the suite, the police left. Ramona then vacated the apartment and made her way to the basement car park where she was pleased to find no police blocking the exits. She jumped into her rental car and left at speed, colliding with the exit barrier as she did so. Once on the freeway, she headed to a friend's house in Sydney's North Shore to borrow a phone.

Meanwhile, Wright was still up on the sixty-first floor of the Meriton Towers holding a large laptop computer while the police circled. At one point he hid in the toilets—literally stood motionless on a toilet bowl in an intentionally unlocked cubicle—as the police searched the area. When he heard no more sound, he then made his way to the service stairs where he received a call from his wife her on her friend's phone.

"She wanted to meet me," Wright recalls, "but I told her I couldn't leave the building."

"At some point I got a call from Craig to say that he was hiding out in the stairwell of the apartment building," Stefan Matthews recalls. "He told me he'd been there for hours and that he had no way of knowing whether the police had left the building or not. He didn't know what to do."

Unsure what to do either, Matthews drove to the DeMorgan offices in North Ryde where the officials were still trying to harvest whatever data they could. Thinking on his feet, Matthews contacted John Laxon at the criminal law firm Laxon Lex to seek urgent advice about Wright's position.

"I was told there was nothing stopping Craig from leaving the country. They more or less told me that's exactly what he should do until the situation calmed down," Matthews recalls

Matthews then contacted Ramona and arranged to meet her at a coffee shop they both knew in the Chatswood Shopping Center, which was midway between downtown Sydney and the Wrights' former home in Gordon. There they discussed the next moves and it was agreed that Ramona would deal with the kids and Matthews would handle Craig.

Ramona bought her husband a ticket on the first available flight to an international destination, which turned out to be Auckland, New Zealand. Later that afternoon, having finally left the apartment building after several hours evading police, an exhausted Craig Wright texted his wife and suggested they too meet.

"I've booked you a flight to Auckland," Ramona told her paranoid and shaken husband.

"But I don't have my passport," Wright told her. "It's still in the apartment."

Worried that she'd be arrested if she returned to the apartment, it was decided that Wright would go to the airport and wait. Meanwhile, Ramona's friend would return to the apartment for the passport, which they did, while also retrieving another laptop and a power chord.

They met Wright at the airport car park where she handed him his passport, another laptop, and $600 cash she'd withdrawn from an ATM. Wright meanwhile—tired, unshaven, and scared with just the yellow bag he'd bought at the airport to carry two laptops, to his name—boarded a flight to Auckland on a one-way ticket. When he'd see his wife and kids again, he had no idea.

"Most people don't understand that the raid had nothing whatsoever to do with me leaving Australia and coming to London," says Wright. "I was already living in London—that's what people don't get. Why do you think the police raided my empty house?"

CHAPTER **NINE**

Proof?

When Craig Wright arrived in Auckland, using airport WiFi, the first person he contacted was Stefan Matthews on Skype audio.

The plan was to get Wright to Manila where Matthews would arrive two days later following a flight out of Sydney via Hong Kong. Matthews arranged the ticket and told Wright to meet him at Terminal 3 in Ninoy Aquino International Airport.

Wright arrived into Terminal 3 an hour before Matthews arrived at Terminal 2. It took Matthews a further hour to reach Terminal 3 in his car with his driver due to extreme traffic.

"Craig was calling me every ten minutes saying 'Where are you?'" Matthews remembers. "He seemed highly stressed, and understandably so."

Once at Terminal 3, Matthews called Wright. "What are you wearing?" he asked.

"I'm in a yellow T-shirt, and I'm wearing a white beach hat," Wright told him. A habitual suit wearer, Wright had purchased some uncharacteristically casual clothes at Auckland Airport as a means of remaining low-key. He knew all too well that his face would be everywhere. Newspaper stories had said that he was trying to flee Australia.

PROOF?

The two met and Matthews drove Wright to his home in Manila and ejected his kids from their room to allow his friend to take it. Matthews's kids had heard of Craig Wright and had seemingly been excited to meet their father's now famous friend.

"Craig spent most of the night talking to my kids about Bitcoin," Matthews remembers. In the morning, they came to me and said, 'Dad, this guy is awesome.'"

That day, Matthews took Wright to buy some more formal clothes prior to a flight to London a few days later. Meanwhile, there was a plot twist evolving regarding the *WIRED* and *Gizmodo* stories. And it was a juicy one.

Seemingly, within twenty-four hours of going public with the articles outing Wright as Satoshi Nakamoto, the journalists involved were already starting to have serious doubts about what they'd sent to print.

So-called experts out in the Bitcoin world had predictably dog-piled onto the details of the pieces as soon as they broke. Not only that, some had cherry-picked the evidence presented by the articles and had contacted the writers with what they claimed to be errors and alternate versions of events.

Faced with this worrying news, the writers (none of whom responded to my emails) perhaps became nervous, and understandably so. Two days after their big reveals, they must have been wondering whether it was *they* who had been tricked by their sources. Events were evolving quickly. By December 11th, both publications had issued follow-up stories amending the originals.

"New Clues Suggest Craig Wright, Suspected Bitcoin Creator, May Be a Hoaxer," the *WIRED* article said.

"The Mystery of Craig Wright and Bitcoin Isn't Solved Yet," *Gizmodo*'s update stated.

"Again, I was contacted by one of the journalists who'd seen me posting on Twitter," says Grigg. "Again, I didn't reply."

Central to the publications' doubts was specific feedback they'd received about several aspects of the original articles' claims, the first of which related to the PGP keys referenced in the apparent draft of an agreement from 2008 between Wright and Dave Kleiman where the latter was to be given 1.1 million bitcoin.

And then there were the questions being raised about the validity of Wright's doctorate from Charles Sturt University, the existence of a super-computer he was rumored to have purchased at huge cost from a US company called SGI who were saying they'd never heard of his company. As if that wasn't enough, there were various aspects of Wright's history where people were saying that he'd made retrospective changes to documents to make it appear that he was more involved with the invention of Bitcoin than he had been.

As far as the PGP matter was concerned, it was the most potentially damaging for Wright.

Sarah Jeong—a contributor on *Vice*'s Motherboard site—was claiming, apparently based on information provided by the aforementioned Bitcoin development engineer Greg Maxwell, who perhaps has his own reasons, that the PGP keys were backdated—in effect created *after* 2008 but made to look as if they had an earlier origin date. If this was the case, Maxwell, who had his own reasons to discredit Wright relating to his founding role in Bitcoin's main competitor Blockstream, was arguing that Craig Wright couldn't therefore be Satoshi Nakamoto.

"If I came back as Satoshi, the whole game plan was over for these people," Wright says.

Confronted with this new "evidence," the many people who didn't want Craig Wright to be Satoshi Nakamoto were probably delighted. Indeed, many would have simply accepted the Motherboard story as fact and moved on in the certainty that the whole outing of Wright was bogus. The problem was that the Motherboard piece would later turn out to be wrong.

PROOF?

Meanwhile, Ian Grigg and his informal Prometheus project assistants were also perpetuating the idea that the *WIRED* and *Gizmodo* stories were inaccurate. But they were doing so for totally different reasons than those presented by Wright's detractors.

Wright's haters claimed the articles' findings were false because they believed that Wright couldn't possibly be Satoshi, nor did they want him to be. Project Prometheus on the other hand was sowing doubt not because they thought the articles' contents were wrong, but because they knew that the publications had gotten the stories pretty much *right*.

By running clever but subtle interference on social media, Grigg and Prometheus were simply trying to buy Craig Wright time to get out of Australia and to London.

"We had to be careful to debunk without actually saying what we knew or telling any lies," recalls Grigg.

As it turned out, Wright hardly needed Project Prometheus's help to rubbish the *WIRED* and *Gizmodo* articles. By the time he reached the safety of London, it was if the world had already dismissed the idea that he was the inventor of Bitcoin.

Inevitably, suggestions surfaced that the outing of Wright had been an inside job orchestrated by Wright and his team. In other words, the documents had been leaked to begin a process of recognizing Wright as Satoshi and pushing him out there as a genius for commercial gain.

"Why would I do that?" Wright says. "Pretty much everything that *WIRED* and *Gizmodo* had looked horrible from my point of view. Documents were doctored to make me look bad. If I was going to leak information about myself, I'd want to make sure the information made me look good."

Even Wright's explanation wasn't enough for some who believed that the leaking of damning information itself was just a predictable double bluff on Wright's part, done only to make it appear as if he *couldn't* have outed himself. Either way, Wright couldn't win.

Whatever the facts were, what was true was that, in December 2015, the only people who were seemingly unfazed by the whole outing debacle were the people associated with nCrypt, all of whom steamed forward with their plans.

"Craig flew on to London, and by that stage, Ramona had also made her way to London," Stefan Matthews says. "And then Craig, Ramona, Rob, and the rest of the team all met, and I believe now that Andrew O'Hagan was also present. I didn't even know O'Hagan existed until I got to London in January of 2016."

The Scottish author Andrew O'Hagan came into the Craig Wright story after being approached, at the request of Robert MacGregor, and asked whether he'd be interested in writing a book about Satoshi Nakamoto, and by extension, documenting the birth of the new company nChain.

Seemingly, MacGregor had specifically chosen O'Hagan because he'd been impressed with his previous work and thought he'd be an accurate biographer capable of capturing events as they evolved.

"O'Hagan was Rob's idea, and he was brought in as the official company biographer as far as I understood it. Rob told me there was a contract, even showed me a contract, but I later found out that he never actually got O'Hagan to sign the damn thing," Wright says.

The initial approach had apparently come a few weeks prior to Wright's outing in Australia and the reason it came at all was because there was a minor clause in the deal signed on June 29th, 2015, whereby life story rights had been acquired from the person (Craig Wright) behind the Satoshi Nakamoto pseudonym.

After researching the basic background of the story a little, O'Hagan, who had previously collaborated with WikiLeaks founder Julian Assange on a somewhat troublesome memoir in 2011, first met Robert MacGregor in London on Thursday November 12th, almost a month before the majority of the world knew anything about Craig Wright's role in Bitcoin.

"He was forty-seven but looked about twenty-nine," O'Hagan said of MacGregor in his *London Review of Books* story, which was published on June 30th, 2016.

In the meeting, MacGregor told O'Hagan that if he agreed to participate he would be given full access to the whole story and all the people in Wright's world.

"MacGregor described Wright to me as 'the goose that lays the golden egg,'" O'Hagan said in the piece.

It was further presented to O'Hagan by MacGregor that the culmination of the story would be Wright proving once and for all that he was Satoshi Nakamoto by using cryptographic keys that only Satoshi had access to—the keys associated with the very first blocks in the blockchain.

"He said it would be 'game over,'" O'Hagan wrote.

Andrew O'Hagan first met Craig and Ramona Wright for lunch at a wine bar and restaurant called 28°–50° in Marylebone on December 16th, 2015, three days after the Wrights had made their way separately to London. Robert MacGregor was also present that afternoon.

O'Hagan describes the couple as being unremarkable, almost as if they were a pair of carefree holidaymakers passing through London, and represents Wright as awkward and sheepish, reluctant to make eye contact.

Two days later, a second meeting was scheduled and the plan was to finally sign off on the papers that would rubber stamp the term sheet that had been hurriedly drawn up back in Sydney in June. At this second meeting, it was explained to everyone present that all of the intellectual property owned by Wright's companies, and by Wright himself, would formally belong to the new company. This would allow Wright's patents to be rolled out quickly in response to a gathering awareness about the value of the blockchain among large banks, some of which were already trying to create their own versions. It was an arms race, basically—and MacGregor wanted to get ahead of his enemies. O'Hagan meanwhile embarked on a working relationship with Wright that would continue for several months.

"I went to London in early January of 2016," Stefan Matthews recalls. "It was then that MacGregor said to me for the first time, 'Okay, this is the plan. We need to get Craig onstage, we need to do public proofs, we need to turn him into a fucking Steve Jobs.'"

In the aftermath of Wright's reputation being summarily trashed by the tech world, Robert MacGregor wasn't of a mind to ditch his man as many might have in the face of the kind of widespread ridicule being directed Wright's way. Instead, MacGregor was doubling down, adamant that all of the accusations against Wright could be disproved and everything would be cool. One way or another, he would show to the world that Craig Wright was Satoshi Nakamoto.

"The computer technology world had dismissed him after the *WIRED* 'outing' of him in December 2015, but Wright and the company just marched on, with the help of an expensive PR company, preparing for the big reveal that would prove the naysayers wrong," Andrew O'Hagan wrote, again for *London Review of Books*.

The only person who didn't buy into the plan as it was now being presented was Craig Wright. He just wanted to work, to create patents and for his life to carry on as if the *WIRED* and *Gizmodo* articles had never happened. The last thing Wright wanted was an image consultant, fashion makeover, and to be pushed out there to prove to the world who he really was at TED talks, as was apparently being proposed.

"As far as I was concerned, my end of the deal was to create a specific number of patents," Wright says. "But Rob wanted something else."

"Craig and MacGregor had some of the all-time great donnybrooks around a boardroom table that you could ever imagine," Stefan Matthews recalls. "And I was caught in the middle."

On one hand, Matthews was the guy who Wright trusted so much but who at the same time he was saying to him, "Stefan, you understand I don't want to do this and you understand why." Meanwhile, Matthews had Robert MacGregor in his other ear saying, "Stefan, you know he *has* to do this and you know why."

"I was fucked, whichever way I moved," Matthews says.

As time passed, apparently MacGregor became increasingly anxious and heavy-handed, to the point where he began to imply that if Wright didn't follow the plan that was being laid out for him, he was walking away from the deal altogether. The reason for this stance was that sometime during January of 2016—perhaps because of the fallout from the outing of Wright in the press—MacGregor's vision for the business had seemingly altered.

"Robert MacGregor's interaction with me personally changed," Matthews recalls. "Looking back now, I'm not certain what his plan ever was. But, at the time, it appeared to me that, by the end of January 2016, he changed his focus and he wanted to flip the business rather than keep it. He wanted to sell the IP and sell the business, whereas previously he'd never had those discussions with me at all. He was suggesting a completely different thing."

The situation had gone from one where they set up the office, hired staff, and worked on the original plan as was discussed in June 2015, to one where Craig Wright was to be revealed as Satoshi Nakamoto and then he and his IP would be packaged up as a "brand" and sold to an entity like Google or Uber, both of which had apparently been approached and initial conversations had taken place.

"Rob saw everything from the perspective of a businessman. He'd put so much in, so he wanted so much out. He wanted to flip the business and I had no interest in doing that. The last people I wanted to sell to was fucking Google. I hate Silicon Valley. It's a shit show that should be burned to the ground," Wright says.

Wright and MacGregor were at a critical impasse. As far as Wright saw things, he was in the process of creating a micro-payments system that could undermine companies like Google and Facebook—entities that relied on an advertising model for revenue. Wright just couldn't get his head around why anyone would want to sell his invention—an invention that rendered the advertising model obsolete—to those very companies.

"What do you think they'd have done with my invention? Jack Dorsey at Twitter wanted to make a fucking ad version of what I was doing and that was everything I hated," says Wright.

Wright was taking a stand for Bitcoin, and wasn't prepared to let his work be sold out to businesses he despised for the sake of a lot of money. Indeed, he would rather have been poor and retained some integrity than be paid a billion dollars to make a deal with what he saw as the devil in Silicon Valley.

With tensions rising over what the next steps should be, Wright found himself anxious and with few allies other than his wife Ramona, who was becoming increasingly anxious on her husband's behalf.

"I should have listened to Ramona more," Wright reflects. "She never trusted Rob."

Stefan Matthews, as much as he was Wright's friend and confidante, had half a foot in Wright's camp and one and a half feet in Rob MacGregor's, where the deal lay. Calvin Ayre, meanwhile, was still in exile and only able to observe from a distance.

"I was just sitting down there in Antigua in my own little bubble," Ayre says. "I knew Craig and Rob MacGregor were like oil and water. But, at the time, I didn't get the impression from Craig that he had a problem with the direction the plans were going in. For whatever reason, he never voiced those concerns to me."

Matthews, Wright, and Ayre met at Ayre's house in Antigua in February of 2016 and the plan was apparently to have a frank and honest face-to-face about what the next steps would be.

"It was an opportunity for the three of us to spend a few relaxing days together and to talk about the business," Matthews remembers.

What came out of the conversations was that—no matter what ultimately happened with packaging up the business and selling it—*nothing* would happen unless Wright could categorically prove that he was Satoshi Nakamoto. As much as Ayre, Matthews, and MacGregor believed him, few others did. Indeed, as it turned out, even Andrew O'Hagan was still on the fence after a few months of occupying Craig Wright's mind. In fact, the reason that he hadn't yet signed a contract or an NDA was that he refused to do so until he too had cast iron proof that Wright's Satoshi claims were true. He couldn't in good faith write a book without it, he told them. Clearly, this lack of definitive proof was the elephant in the room that most needed to be addressed.

In the interim, the accusations against Wright claiming he was a fraud in the revised *Gizmodo* and *WIRED* stories had at least been rebuffed in one way or another, in a manner that was just about satisfactory. The *VICE* Motherboard accusation about the backdated PGP key was eviscerated by an impressive paper authored by Dr. Nick Sharples BSc (Hons) DPhil and Dave Kilroy BSc (Hons) MSc, both experts in the cryptography field. The conclusion of the detailed report was that Greg Maxwell's assessment, reported in the article, that said the two PGP keys could not have been created in 2008, was wrong.

Similarly, the accusations that Wright's company Cloudcroft had no relationship with SGI, the US-based super-computer company who sold him hardware, was semi-debunked when Wright produced a signed NDA dated December 5th, 2014, which clearly showed that Wright's companies DeMorgan Ltd. and Panopticrypt Pty Ltd. (not Cloudcroft, however) had an agreement with SGI—an agreement that Wright says SGI didn't want publicly known.

"Cloudcroft didn't have the agreement," Wright says, "But SGI knew very well that Cloudcroft had an internal contract with DeMorgan. They didn't lie, but they did mislead people. And the reason they did was because SGI is a US company, and technically, because they were selling me computers that were linked into gaming, they were breaching US embargo rules. They knew I was involved with poker. Strange what people will do for money. So, they basically covered things up because they didn't want to get in trouble."

As for the other claim against him made in the magazines' follow up pieces, Charles Sturt University provided a photocopy of Wright's staff card proving he'd lectured there and Wright himself was able to rustle up a draft thesis from somewhere that he says he'd submitted for the doctorate it was claimed he didn't have. What was left hanging was whether Wright's thesis was actually approved.

Not that it mattered. When submitted to the court of public opinion, none of these rebuttals changed anyone's mind. In fact, no matter what evidence he came up with, Craig Wright was viewed as a laughing stock and a fraud. The only way to change the tide of opinion was to do what he absolutely didn't want to do: cryptographically prove he was Satoshi Nakamoto.

PROOF?

The definitive way to do this, and the *only* way to appease Wright's peers in the cryptography world and indeed anyone else who cared, would be if Wright signed a transaction using the private key from one of Satoshi's original blocks. Anything less just wasn't going to cut it, and so it was agreed in Antigua that as part of a series of "proof sessions" that were scheduled to take place sometime in April 2016, two respected figures from the Bitcoin world, and Jon Matonis, would be invited to the UK to fulfil the role of reliable witnesses.

Matonis and Andresen were logical choices. In 2010, Andresen had been appointed by Satoshi Nakamoto himself as the lead developer of the reference implementation for Bitcoin client software when Nakamoto left the scene. Two years later, Andresen was appointed chief scientist of the Bitcoin Foundation for whom Jon Matonis was a founding director. Both were highly respected figures within the Bitcoin community. Neither had agendas of their own.

While Andresen claimed that he hadn't even heard of Craig Wright prior to being approached to be part of the Satoshi proof sessions, Jon Matonis certainly had. Indeed, while attending a Bitcoin conference in June of 2015 in Sydney, he arranged to meet Wright, who he only knew at the time as a fellow Bitcoin advocate, for a coffee.

In a blog article about the meeting published in 2016, Matonis wrote: *"After discussing many technical and economic aspects of the current Bitcoin protocol debates, I returned to my hotel room after an exhausting day. I remember saying to my wife that I had this weird feeling of having just met Satoshi."*

Both Matonis and especially Andresen were wary about what the proof sessions might mean. As much as Craig Wright's reputation would be on the line, theirs would be too. And damaged reputations are hard to fix in the cryptography world. They knew all too well that any ambiguity would be ruthlessly pounced upon.

Nevertheless, Andresen was contacted in March of 2016 by a PR company, The Outside Organisation, that had been tasked with managing all aspects of the Satoshi proof sessions, which also included arranging for Craig Wright to be given media training, specifically in terms of how to answer questions and how not to answer them. This media training was given throughout March and April by another London-based outfit called Milk Publicity.

While email communication between Andresen and Wright took place over a few days, as requested by Andresen as one of his conditions for engaging with the proof process, it was agreed that Wright would first do with Andrew O'Hagan in private what he was later going to do with Andresen and Matonis. He would sign with the private key from one of Satoshi's original blocks.

On a sunny morning in April, Andrew O'Hagan showed up at Wright's house on the appointed day when it was to be proven to him beyond doubt that Craig Wright, the man he'd been talking to almost daily for four months, was Satoshi Nakamoto, the inventor of Bitcoin.

In his *London Review of Books* story, O'Hagan described an awkward Wright, bathed in cologne and unable to make small talk. Wright made O'Hagan a cup of tea, and led him into a study where there were three computers and seven screens

"There were rows of computing books and seven dead laptops stacked on top a bookshelf," O'Hagan wrote.

Wright then explained to O'Hagan what the Genesis block is, that it was hardcoded and not mined like every subsequent block would be. Wright then explained that he was going to send O'Hagan a message from the first mined address on the blockchain. With that, Wright then typed the words "Here I am, Andrew" onto a keyboard. And then he verified the signature.

"I shook his hand. Then I stared at the screen and considered how strange it would be to live with a secret for seven years and then feel no relief when it finally came out," O'Hagan wrote.

Not quite sure what he'd just witnessed in a moment of profound anti-climax, O'Hagan asked Wright to explain in layperson's terms what he'd just done.

"I just digitally signed a message using the first ever mined address on Bitcoin," Wright told him.

O'Hagan described how in that moment, any doubts he'd had about Wright being Satoshi, pretty much melted away.

"It wasn't merely that Wright had been in the right place at the right time; he had been in the only place at the only time…" he wrote.

"They want the most convoluted explanation. But they can say what they want; I've got nothing more to prove," Wright told O'Hagan, seemingly buoyed by what he'd just done.

Meanwhile, in the background, Wright had been communicating with Gavin Andresen by email and Andresen had been asking Wright probing questions in an attempt to ascertain whether the person he was communicating with was the same person he'd been emailing back in 2009. Wright was compliant and forthcoming, and even sent Andresen an email as "himself," followed by another with similar content written as Satoshi would have written it. The two discussed the history of Bitcoin and mathematical theory over a number of emails. Wright even alluded to some major errors that he thought he'd made in some highly revealing email communications with Andresen.

"At some point I actually thought I'd missed some important opportunities to scale Bitcoin," Wright explains. "I thought it was possible that Bitcoin could have failed at several points in its history. After all the effort I'd put in in Australia between 2011 and

2015, I thought nobody would listen to me. Let's just say that 2015 wasn't my most optimistic time."

Wright also sent Andresen some in-progress research papers he was working on at that time. Andresen reported that the "Satoshi" email had sounded like the Satoshi he had worked with years previously and that the papers matched his academic, "math-heavy" tone as well.

What mattered even more was that Andresen was sufficiently satisfied and curious enough to get on a plane to London, all expenses paid by MacGregor and Matthews, to meet Wright in person ahead of the big proof exercise that everyone hoped would change the world. He left Boston and landed at London Heathrow on the morning of April 7th and checked himself in at the Covent Garden Hotel. He went to his room, grabbed a couple of hours sleep, and then went downstairs to meet Robert MacGregor and Stefan Matthews. When Craig Wright showed up a little later, he and Andresen apparently got along very well, just as they had done by email. Wright was clearly emotional about what he was about to do, but in a fellow mathematician's company he was comparatively relaxed.

Meanwhile, Stefan Matthews had booked a large conference room in the hotel's basement, and it was here, far away from the outside world, that the proof session would take place.

"Craig knew what was at stake," Matthews says. "He wasn't about to prove who he was to just anyone; he was proving who he was to someone in the Bitcoin industry who he knew everyone would believe and respect. Craig knew this was it."

What followed was, by all accounts, a drawn-out and confusing series of events where Wright and Andresen talked at length while one (Andresen) scribbled notes and the other (Wright) stared at a computer screen while talking about the history of Bitcoin and his plans for its future.

Eventually, at around 5:30 p.m., the moment of proof arrived. Craig Wright sighed, adjusted his chair and logged onto his laptop to prepare to sign a message as Satoshi Nakamoto with the key and have it verified as Andresen watched from his side.

The message was signed and duly verified.

Anyone who was in the room at the time says that it was quite a profound moment, and that Andresen seemed more than a little overwhelmed not simply by what he'd just witnessed, but also by the fact that he could finally acknowledge that he was actually in the same room with Satoshi Nakamoto, the person who'd entrusted him with so much responsibility back in 2011.

But it wasn't really over. There was one more step.

To be doubly sure of what he'd just witnessed and to rule out any fraud or sleight of hand, Andresen requested that the signing process be done not just on Wright's computer, but also on his own, which he unpacked from a bag by his side while at the same time removing a new USB stick from its packaging. Andresen's argument was that Wright's laptop could have been "pre-loaded" with everything that was needed to complete the signing. He stopped short of suggesting that Wright could somehow have tricked him. To address this concern, he suggested that the key could be used on *his* laptop and then saved to the USB stick that he would then give Wright to keep.

Wright didn't like this idea at all. In his mind, he'd just signed a message to one of the most respected men in Bitcoin as Satoshi and now even that wasn't enough.

"You do one thing; they want two. You do two; they want three. The goalposts just kept getting moved," says Wright.

Apparently, Wright got up from the table and started walking around the room muttering darkly. As much as he trusted Andresen, he had promised himself he would never let the private key go or show it in public. Now, he was being asked to do the former, and he was digging his heels in in opposition.

"I do not want to categorically prove keys across machines," he had written in an email to Andrew O'Hagan sometime earlier.

Wright started backing off and suggesting he and Andresen take things slowly like they were a couple who'd gotten ahead of themselves on a first date. He said that maybe they should just resume sending each other emails again. Wright even offered to do a few more message signings like the one he'd just done.

Rob MacGregor and Stefan Matthews meanwhile were boiling over with frustration in another corner of the conference room. Perhaps they sensed the "game over" plan was slipping away. They thought Andresen's request to carry out a little more due-diligence was entirely reasonable given the circumstances. He'd come this far, got on a flight; he only wanted to see the exercise through and be done with it all. Equally, they thought Wright was being unnecessarily obstinate, especially given what was at stake for everyone in the room. In their eyes, Wright was refusing to do the one thing he knew would end all of the doubts: the "game over" moment MacGregor had talked about before.

It was a tense standoff, but one thing was certain: they sure as hell weren't going to let Gavin Andresen leave and get on a plane with the whole process hanging in the balance. One way or another, they were determined to come up with a solution that both satisfied him and appeased Wright's considerable paranoia about losing control of his private keys, and by extension, his Satoshi alter ego. With neither party trusting each other's hardware, Stefan Matthews came up with what he thought was a perfect compromise position: a brand-new piece of hardware that belonged to neither of them, straight out of the box.

At six p.m., Matthews called his assistant and told her to go out and find a brand-new laptop computer from wherever she could get one at such a late hour. Half an hour later, a brand-new laptop in an unopened box was duly delivered to the Covent Garden Hotel. The new computer was unboxed, set up, and connected to the hotel's WiFi so that software could be loaded on that would allow the signing procedure to happen via an Electrum wallet.

While this was being done, Wright's mood darkened further while he fretted and ranted about being bullied by "the businessmen in the room," as he called them, presumably referring to Mac-Gregor and Matthews, who were grimacing in unison across the room while texting furiously.

"Craig was on the edge," Matthews recalls. "We knew what he needed to do, but we had no idea if he was going to go through with it."

Somebody suggested that Wright should call his wife Ramona for advice. He did, and when she answered and he explained his situation and what, specifically, he was now being asked to do, her response suggested that even she was resigned to the inevitable. "Just do it," she told him.

Wright used the new laptop to open the relevant Electrum wallet so that he could sign the definitive message from Satoshi to Gavin Andresen. If he did it, everything would be over and Andresen could get on a plane while everyone else could walk off into the sunset on an eternal victory lap. However, the initial attempt to sign the message failed. The message did not verify. Wright tried it three more times and on each occasion it failed again. Then, Andresen, despite being weary from just two hours of sleep, noticed that Wright had omitted the initials CSW at the end of the message whereas he'd used them in the original. Sure enough, when Wright tried again with CSW tagged on the end, the message verified. Craig Wright had just demonstrated on a computer straight from the box that he had the ability to sign a message to Gavin Andresen with Satoshi's private key.

Wright was left an emotional wreck by the day's events. Apparently, he had tears in his eyes and could barely form the words required to say to Rob MacGregor and Stefan Matthews that he was sorry for being a little awkward.

"I could tell it had taken a lot out of him," Matthews recalls. "He kept saying that he never thought he'd have to do what he'd just done. But he did it."

Andresen was so exhausted that he departed to bed. Wright, Matthews, and MacGregor were equally wiped out, but also relieved.

"I could see what Craig had been through," Matthews says. "I couldn't just put him in a taxi and send him home. Instead, we all went off to find a bottle of wine," Matthews laughs.

At some point during late March or April of 2016 (it is unclear exactly when during this time period it occurred) Jon Matonis was present in London for a private signing session similar to the one Andresen witnessed. Matonis wrote about the event in his blog, which was published on May 2nd, 2016.

> "*During the London proof sessions, I had the opportunity to review the relevant data along three distinct lines: cryptographic, social, and technical. Based on what I witnessed, it is my firm belief that Craig Steven Wright satisfies all three categories. For cryptographic proof in my presence, Craig signed and verified a message using the private key from block #1 newly generated coins and from block #9 newly-generated coins (the first transaction to Hal Finney). The social evidence, including his unique personality, early emails that I received, and early drafts of the Bitcoin*

white paper, points to Craig as the creator. I also received satisfactory explanations to my questions about registering the bitcoin.org domain and the various time-of-day postings to the BitcoinTalk forum. Additionally, Craig's technical working knowledge of public key cryptography, Bitcoin's addressing system, and proof-of-work consensus in a distributed peer-to-peer environment is very strong.

According to me, the proof is conclusive and I have no doubt that Craig Steven Wright is the person behind the Bitcoin technology, Nakamoto consensus, and the Satoshi Nakamoto name."

CHAPTER **TEN**

Sartre

As it turned out, the Andresen and Matonis proof sessions were only half of the bigger plan to reveal Satoshi Nakamoto to the world. The events that would unfold over the weeks following Andresen's trip to London were bewildering and complicated. Not only that, they also pushed Craig Wright over the edge.

It was decided that there would be a major press event in early May of 2016 where Wright would formally be unmasked as Satoshi Nakamoto, the inventor of Bitcoin. To coincide with the announcement, which Wright would initially make on his own blog, all of the evidence that debunked the *WIRED* and *Gizmodo* follow-up pieces—the academic paper written about the backdated PGP claim, the response from Charles Sturt University about the doctorate, the proof sessions with Matonis and Andresen and their comments in the aftermath of them, would all be bundled up into one overwhelming mic-drop of evidence that would be presented to selected members of the world's press on a given day in advance of the big announcement. The plan was for this day to be the slam-dunk moment that team Satoshi so desperately wanted and the world at large required.

Wright however, was still unwilling and seemingly became increasingly agitated as the day approached. It became clear that

Wright was having some kind of buyer's remorse. In his urgency to clear his feet of debt in Australia and to fend off what he saw as nothing more than ATO overreach, he had signed up for something he never really wanted to do or believed he would ever really have to do, without giving it too much thought at the time.

"He's sold his soul. That's how simple this is," Allan Pederson, who'd relocated with Wright from Australia to continue his role as Wright's project manager in London, told author Andrew O'Hagan.

Pedersen was speaking from experience, having been around Wright and his business habits in Australia. His view was that, as much as Wright always claimed that he didn't ever want to be outed as Satoshi, there was part of him, a much bigger part, that really did.

"It's in his personality. He wants to be recognized," Pedersen also told O'Hagan.

Wanting to be recognized as Satoshi Nakamoto, and doing what was necessary to back up such a proclamation, were two different things. And it was the latter—proving it—that sat so awkwardly with Wright in the days that led up to the grand performance that was set for early May of 2016.

"I didn't ever want to go down the whole signing publicly bit because it undermined everything I was trying to say. I was sitting there saying 'You don't prove identity with keys.' Identity is fire-walled, but it doesn't mean it doesn't exist," says Wright.

But as hesitant as he might have been and as adamant as he was that he wasn't prepared to keep jumping through hoops for anyone. Wright was powerless and knew it. The truth was that he was being swept along toward peril by a force far more powerful than his own misgivings: the guys in the background for whom failure was simply inconceivable.

Robert MacGregor, in particular, only had eyes for the finish line and was relentless in his desire to drag Wright across it. The moneymen were much too invested in every sense to change course, far less turn back. For them, the only way out was through.

"They believed that only one big thing was going to happen: Craig Wright was going to emerge as Satoshi Nakamoto, the great mystery figure of the digital age, and the evidence would be 'overwhelming,'" O'Hagan wrote, while acknowledging that his own journalistic independence was slipping.

The Outside Agency PR team had contacted a number of outlets and the ones that had shown the most interest in the story were the BBC, *The Economist*, and *GQ* magazine.

Each editor at the publications would have to sign an NDA and would have their stories embargoed until the agreed date when the embargo would be lifted—May 2nd, 2016. In return, they'd each get time with Wright during which he'd demonstrate proof to them by using his Satoshi key. Thereafter, they'd all be allocated time to interview him about what they'd seen and to ask any questions they might have to make their articles as objective as they could be.

As worthy an idea as managing an event of this kind with an old school PR approach was, the two simply didn't belong in the same world. Indeed, many in the cryptocurrency world believed that all Wright really had to do was move a single coin from an early block and it would really be game over.

But this wasn't being offered quite yet. Instead, the press were being micro-managed in combination with being presented with a package of other far less definitive "proofs." If the plan was to make Wright and his claims appear more credible, the result was exactly the opposite.

"I didn't like it, and I told the lawyer: 'You're basically setting up a rock show and Craig is not a rock star,'" Ian Grigg told *CoinGeek* in 2021. "Not only was it the wrong approach for Craig, it was the wrong approach for the industry."

Regardless, the rock show rolled on into town, and on Tuesday, April 25th, at the offices of The Outside Agency on Tottenham Court Road, the scheduled meetings with Wright took place.

Rory Cellan-Jones, Technology Correspondent at the BBC was the first to be invited into a conference room with his producers where Wright sat staring at a laptop screen. Also in the room as observers were Jon Matonis and Rob MacGregor.

"When I was presented to him by this PR agency, I didn't really know anything about Craig Wright," Cellan-Jones says. "Hardly anybody did. I'd heard the Satoshi Nakamoto story broadly, but that's all."

Cellan-Jones, a highly respected and professional journalist was approaching the meeting just like any mainstream journalist would have. He simply wanted to demonstrate to a BBC audience— the kind who might not have known anything about Bitcoin—what the crux of the Satoshi Nakamoto story was. As such, his questions were open and reasonable. Rather than putting Wright in a tight spot, they were inviting him to show himself, and his invention, in the best possible light. Wright, however, did not see it that way at all. From the outset he appeared resentful, irritated, and borderline rude.

After a lengthy preamble, Cellan-Jones asked Wright if he could sign a message for him, and by extension, a BBC audience of millions.

"Hi, historic message to the BBC," Wright typed, while explaining broadly what he was doing, which was that he was signing the message with block 9, the key owned by Satoshi which was used with Hal Finney back in 2009.

"We've seen Craig use a private key known to have been used with Hal Finney. And we've verified it with the public key," Cellan-Jones confirmed aloud.

"Yes," Wright replied.

Wright then went off on a strange tangent about Jean Paul Sartre's speech when the French playwright turned down the Nobel Prize for literature in 1964. Nobody in the room, especially Rory Cellan-Jones, knew where Wright was going with it. As it turned out, Wright's plan was to attach Sartre's speech cryptographically to block 9 of the blockchain and then to verify it publicly on his blog later. Wright then started ranting, saying that he never wanted to sign Craig Wright as Satoshi in the first place. He didn't want to come out, he said. He'd been forced to reveal himself.

Cellan-Jones was confused and asked Wright in what way he felt he'd been pressured. Wright referenced the bailout deal signed in Sydney in June 2015.

"I don't want to be the public face of anything," Wright said to Cellan-Jones when he was asked whether he really wanted to be known as the public face of Bitcoin.

Cellan-Jones's piece was scheduled to go live a few days later. However, there was more, as there always seemed to be. The BBC said they wanted to return the following day to record an interview with Wright on camera, which was something he'd been adamant he would not agree to.

"I was naïve and went along with everything. I just wanted people to leave me alone. As far as the BBC was concerned, the contract I had with them was that there would be no cameras. I would have never agreed to that," Wright says. "But they showed up with bloody cameras. I was made to do it."

"Craig said that I broke an agreement not to film him, which was complete and utter bollocks," Cellan-Jones says. "Just ask yourself: what do you think a TV reporter does? If a PR company had come to me and said, 'We've got Satoshi Nakamoto...but you can't actually film him' what would I have said?"

Prior to the BBC returning for this contested on-camera interview on Wednesday, April 26, Wright conducted an interview on that Tuesday afternoon with Ludwig Siegele of *The Economist.*

Again, Wright signed a message using block 9 and had the private key verified. Siegele, however, was skeptical and asked Wright what he had actually proved. Wright told him what he thought should have been obvious: that it meant he was in possession of all the original private keys. Seemingly satisfied, Siegele then asked Wright why he'd waited almost eight years to reveal himself and why he ever felt the need to conceal his identity at all. Wright became defensive and told Siegele that he never wanted to be a public figure and that he hoped people wouldn't ever listen to him as Craig Wright.

"They will look at the facts, not decide based on what Satoshi says," he told Siegele, more than a little cryptically.

Later that afternoon, after having photos taken for the *GQ* article, Wright met with the magazine's senior editor Stuart McGurk, who brought along a Polish cryptography expert by the name of Dr. Nicolas Courtois. What followed was nothing short of a debacle. Courtois questioned every claim that Wright made and even countered with theories of his own. In turn, believing his intelligence was being challenged, Wright saw red and started hurling four-letter obscenities back at Courtois. McGurk, meanwhile, was stuck in the middle, and to his immense credit, remained extraordinarily calm in his attempts to keep the conversation civilized. But Wright, by this point, was too far gone. Courtois was escorted from the room to the refrain of Wright yelling: "Fuck off!"

"They brought some wanker in," Wright reflects. "And I don't take kindly to wankers."

"Unfortunately, I wasn't there," laughs Stefan Matthews.

The next day, the BBC returned with a full camera crew while Wright, now seething about having to jump through yet another hoop, sat looking unimpressed and uncooperative.

"So, who are you, and what are you about to show me?" Rory Cellan-Jones opened the conversation with.

"My name is Craig Wright, and I'm about to demonstrate the signing of a message with a key that is associated with the first transaction ever done on Bitcoin—a transaction of ten bitcoin to Hal Finney."

"And who did that first transaction?" Cellan-Jones asked.

"I did," Wright replied.

"And whose name is associated with that transaction?"

"The moniker is Satoshi Nakamoto."

Cellan-Jones then zeroed in for real.

"So, you're going to show me that Satoshi Nakamoto…is you?" he asked.

There was a pause.

"I was struck by how nervous and vaguely Asperger's he was. I thought he was deeply weird," Cellan-Jones remembers of Wright's demeanor.

"Yes," Wright finally confirmed.

"Are you confident that this will prove to the world that you are Satoshi?" Cellan-Jones continued.

"It proves I have keys…other things we'll be releasing will help…some people will believe and some won't, and to tell you the truth, I don't really care," Wright said.

Cellan-Jones wasn't finished.

"As weird as it was, I was totally focused on not letting the story end before getting answers. That had been my job for thirty years: making complex stories accessible," Cellan-Jones remembers.

"But can you say, hand on heart, I am Satoshi Nakamoto?" Cellan-Jones asked Wright.

Cellan-Jones had just asked Wright the question he least wanted to answer in the entire world. And he answered it as if it was the question he least wanted to answer in the entire world.

"I was the main part of it. Other people helped," Wright famously said.

"At that moment, I thought *what the fuck*? We'd been approached by the PR organization saying they 'had' Satoshi and as a result my main focus had been to get him to say that he was Satoshi Nakamoto. When he didn't quite give me that answer, I just accepted that what I got was as good as I was going to get," Cellan-Jones reflects.

In that moment, Wright blew the Satoshi Nakamoto myth wide open to the public, while at the same time confirming what Ian Grigg and others had known for some time. It appeared as if Wright couldn't definitively say he was Satoshi Nakamoto because Satoshi Nakamoto never really was one person. It was a team, each with different inputs at different moments in the history of Bitcoin, but a team, nevertheless.

"All I knew was that he presented us with what he said was proof. You'd have to be a much more expert cryptographer than I was to be able to understand. At the time, I was on the fence," Cellan-Jones says.

On the morning of May 2nd, 2016, the press embargo was lifted and the stories winged their way out to the world.

The official line was that Wright had chosen to proclaim himself publicly to be Satoshi in direct response to misleading information that had been circulating since December 2015. Essentially, he was setting the record straight and hoping all the negativity and suspicion would be swept away in a tsunami of overwhelming evidence.

It started very well.

At eight a.m. Wright posted a spurious blog on his own website about Jean Paul Sartre that nobody other than him really understood while at the same time proclaiming to the world that he was Satoshi Nakamoto. He wrote:

> *"Be assured, just as you have worked, I have not been idle during these many years. Since those early days, after distancing myself from the public persona that was Satoshi, I have poured every measure of myself into research. I have been silent, but I have not been absent. I have been engaged with an exceptional group and look forward to sharing our remarkable work when they are ready. Satoshi is dead. But this is only the beginning."*

Thereafter, there was a lengthy explanation of the verification process that explained hashing, public keys, signing, and signature verification accompanied by a number of screenshots of computer code to illustrate what he was saying.

At the same time, Gavin Andresen posted a message to his blog that read:

> *"I believe Craig Steven Wright is the person who invented Bitcoin.*
>
> *I was flown to London to meet Dr. Wright a couple of weeks ago, after an initial email conversation convinced me that there was a very good chance he was the same person I'd communicated with in 2010 and early 2011. After spending time with him I am convinced beyond a reasonable doubt: Craig Wright is Satoshi."*

And that wasn't all. Ian Grigg, a man with considerable inside knowledge also wrote, while continuing to push the "team" theory:

"Craig Wright has just outed himself as the leader of the Satoshi Nakamoto team. I confirm that this is true, both from direct knowledge and a base of evidence."

Around the same time, tweets appeared from Calvin Ayre and *The Economist*. Ten minutes later, Cellan-Jones's report went out on Radio 4's *Today* program. Everything was syncing like clockwork.

Within an hour or so, the internet was blowing up with the name Craig Wright. The name was typed into Google thousands of times. Meanwhile, the mainstream outlets—none of whom knew much about Bitcoin and far less about Satoshi Nakamoto—seemed cautiously impressed by what they were hearing. Craig Wright seemed plausible. The PR machine was creating the right kind of momentum, it appeared.

In the background, however, the cryptography world and the Reddit forums—the people who knew all there was to know about Bitcoin and had been tracking Satoshi's every move since 2008—were ominously silent.

The reason?

Experts and amateur Bitcoin super-sleuths were hard at work on the granular content of Wright's blog post.

Nothing that happened thereafter was good for Craig Wright or the bigger nCrypt plan. Several eagle-eyed researchers had analyzed Wright's blog and had established that what Wright had written was faked. The claim was that something he said had been signed with a Satoshi key had actually been cut and pasted from an old signature that had been available to anyone on the internet for years.

"When we put the piece out on the bank holiday Monday, within a couple of hours, people at a conference in New York were tearing it apart," Rory Cellan-Jones remembers. "Again, I couldn't be certain about who was right and who was wrong, but a substantial number of that incredibly partisan community thought Craig Wright was a fraud."

Out in the cryptography world, the knives were out for Craig Wright. And they were longer and sharper than they'd ever been in 2015. Being outed against his will was one thing, faking his own proof publicly was entirely another. To many in the cryptography world, his actions amounted to heresy.

"People don't realize that I wasn't running my own blog," Wright says. "I wrote one thing and then Rob's staff had it changed. I then said fuck off and they put up this thing about what I was going to do. They said, 'You've already said it to the world, so you'll have to do it.' I said, 'No, I fucking haven't, you did.' But it was on my site with my name and my picture. I could hardly take it back."

Over in New York, five hours behind, at a Blockchain conference called Consensus 2016 that was being held at the Marriot Marquis on Broadway in Manhattan, the initial response had been positive. It was the opening morning of the three-day event when the news about Satoshi's unmasking broke and the delegates at the conference seemed genuinely excited that his identity had finally been revealed. Seemingly, there was a real buzz in the air.

On the panel that day was Gavin Andresen and he duly stood up and confirmed in public more or less what he'd said on his blog a few hours earlier.

"I still believe that Craig Wright is, beyond a reasonable doubt, Satoshi Nakamoto," Andresen announced to an audience of Bitcoiners and speculative investors.

After the conference, when pressed specifically about Wright's faked blog post, Andresen said, "I remind everyone, he is human.

I'm sure he makes mistakes like we all do," he continued. "He's made some mistakes in the past. And he wants his privacy. So I'm going to draw a line. If you ask me questions about this, I draw the line at: I will explain why I'm convinced. I will not go into personal details of the discussion that I had with him."

Not everyone agreed, and one notable dissenter was Vitalik Buterin, the founder of the Bitcoin competitor Ethereum.

"I will explain why I think he's probably not Satoshi," Buterin began, to ripples of applause in an audience of around two hundred.

"He had the opportunity to take two different paths of proving this. One path would have been to make this exact proof, make a signature from the first Bitcoin block, put the signature out in public, make a simple ten-line blog post, so that Dan Boneh [a cryptographer and Stanford University professor] would be convinced and verified...he would let the crypto community verify this. But instead, he has written a huge blog post that is long and confusing, and it has bugs in the software, and he also says he won't release the evidence. Signaling theory says that if you have a good way to prove something and you have a noisy way to do it, then the reason why you picked the noisy way was because you couldn't do it the good way in the first place," Buterin continued.

Gradually, a consensus among Bitcoin core developers started developing that demanded more proof from Wright. They wanted something new signed, and they wanted it done publicly using the Genesis block—a block that was indisputably Satoshi's.

One such developer, Peter Todd, seemingly spoke for all of them when he told *Forbes*, "All Wright needs to do, is to provide a signature on the message that says "Craig Wright is Satoshi Nakamoto" signed by a key known to be Satoshi's. This is really easy to do...if you're actually Satoshi Nakamoto."

With deep resistance and downright anger building in the cryptography world about Wright's faked proof, Rob MacGregor and Stefan Matthews kicked into emergency mode. Rather than backing down, again their plan was to *double* down and to keep doubling down until there was nowhere else to go. The plan now was to give the world precisely what they so wanted. They were going to insist that Craig Wright move Satoshi Bitcoin to prove conclusively that he controlled it, and it was decided that the three logical people he could best move it to and from would be Gavin Andresen, Jon Matonis, and Rory Cellan-Jones of the BBC.

It was agreed that each would first send a small amount of bitcoin to the address used to make the first ever Bitcoin transaction with Hal Finney in 2009. Once received, these coins would then be sent back to the address thus representing the first outgoing transactions since 2009. If Wright could do this, all previous doubts—of which there was a fast-growing deluge—would all be blown away.

On May 3, on his blog, a post appeared with the headline that read "Extraordinary Claims Require Extraordinary Proof" and below it was written the following:

> *"So, over the coming days, I will be posting a series of pieces that will lay the foundations for this extraordinary claim, posting independently-verifiable documents and evidence addressing some of the false allegations that have been levelled, and transferring bitcoin from an early block."*

The next morning, May 4, Wright, reluctant, short of sleep, and desperate, was put in touch with Andresen in New York from his home to discuss how this extraordinary transaction would actually be conducted. His wife Ramona and Stefan Matthews were also there. On the call to Andresen, Wright seemingly expressed concerns about security on the early blockchain. He was most reluctant to proceed.

Basically, Wright thought there was a bug that could potentially leave the transaction open to theft. Andresen, however, having been handed the stewardship of Bitcoin in Satoshi's absence, knew what the deal was. He confirmed that the bug had indeed existed once, but had long since been fixed. Nevertheless, Wright was spiraling downwards in his mind. He was being pushed further and further to do things he just didn't want to do. Something had to give.

And something did.

Once all three of Andresen, Matonis, and Cellan-Jones had sent their small amount of bitcoin to the Satoshi address as requested, the ball was now in Craig Wright's court once and for all. Matonis, Andresen, Cellan-Jones, and the world of Bitcoin waited...

Nothing happened.

At some point in that day, with what he felt was an unreasonable burden of pressure and expectation heaped on him, Wright asked his wife if she could make him a cup of tea. Meanwhile, Wright walked to the bathroom and stood in front of the mirror holding a large knife. Desperate, he cut his own neck several times and slumped back into the shower.

"A couple of minutes after Craig had left the room, there was this hellish scream," Stefan Matthews remembers of that day. "I went to the staircase and Ramona was screaming. I walked up the stairs and into the bathroom. In there was a fourteen-inch blade lying on the toilet seat and blood everywhere on the floor and in the shower. Craig was lying with his upper torso in the shower, fully clothed and unconscious. I grabbed his legs and pulled him out of the shower. Then I grabbed the bath robe and wrapped it around the wounds on his neck while Ramona called an ambulance."

"I don't know..." Wright sighs. "After everyone badgering me and telling what to do, I went up to the bathroom and put a knife in my throat. I'd fairly much lost all concept of the fact that I had a family. All I remember after that was a few flashes from when I was on a gurney and a few bits when I was in the hospital."

"I was at the house a few days later and I saw the marks on his neck. Very disturbing," Andrew O'Hagan recalls of the scene he witnessed.

On the same day, Andresen received an email from Robert Macgregor that read:

"All Stop. Craig has just tried to injure himself and is bleeding badly in the washroom. Stefan is there with him and Ramona and I am en route. Ambulance is on its way."

"I heard about what happened that day," Calvin Ayre says. "For Craig, I'm sure it was real. For me I believe it was a bit of a cry for help. He was clearly having an emotional thing."

Wright indeed felt he'd been pushed over the emotional edge. He felt that Rob MacGregor had put him in an impossible position by telling him that if he didn't move coins as was being suggested, he was pulling all his funding and closing the business down.

"That would have been an endgame. Burning bridges," Wright admits. "I suppose I could have kept plodding along in Australia with a lot of stress. I'd have still been spending half of my fucking life answering the tax office and being frustrated."

The day of Wright's suicide attempt, Robert MacGregor put the brakes on everything. No coins were moved.

By extension, the definitive proof that was so badly needed never happened, and the reason it never happened was because out of nowhere a suggestion surfaced that an issue with the trust that oversaw the Satoshi bitcoins prohibited Wright from moving coins at all. It was rumored that the trustee in question was Wright's own wife Ramona; others suggested it was Uyen Nguyen vetoing things. Both are rumors that have never been substantiated. The intricacies of the trust remain a mystery.

Further, it is unclear exactly who knew about this issue with the trust and when they knew it. One person who certainly did was Ian Grigg. He—in his Project Prometheus capacity—was one of the people responsible for sabotaging the "game over" moment.

"It came out on the Monday and by the Wednesday we had basically decided…not just Craig but me and my mates, the intern, etc., that this was a failure," Grigg told *CoinGeek*. "So, we started to intervene to collapse the tent. One of us put out the word: the trustee says the that the coins must not be moved."

Grigg's reason for intervening was partly personal.

"We saw Craig on camera and we realized things were really bad. He looked shell-shocked. But beyond that we thought that if coins were to be moved, Craig could find himself under a lot of pressure simply because the value of bitcoin was so high at that time. So, in conjunction with the trustee, we put out the message that the coins couldn't move. It wasn't fabricated; it was true," says Grigg.

An article, apparently written by Grigg and posted on the cryptography mailing list on May 4 read:

> *"Finally, as has been reported, the headline bulk of the value is controlled by a trust. Any movement of those coins needs to operate according to trust rules; if not, then we are in a state of sin. What that means is not something that can be described in mathematical terms, but it can certainly be described in hysterical terms—the logic de jour of the Bitcoin community. As an aside, I really strongly suggest that the Bitcoin community not press for the breaking of the trust. If unsure on this point, ask your miners to explain that old curse: 'be careful what you wish for.' Breaking the trust is way off the scale of what anyone will desire."*

"Uyen was part of the Prometheus stuff and I didn't end up agreeing with how that went. I know they said they were trying to help me but they never actually asked me what I wanted. I never wanted to be nominated for awards and all that. It was good intentions, but we all know where they end up…" Wright explains. "In the end, Uyen got nothing from either side and pretty much disappeared thereafter."

Whoever knew about the trust issue, the upshot was that Wright, when pushed to the absolute brink, had been faced with a horrific dilemma that only he understood. Move coins and confirm himself to be Satoshi and perhaps face criminal proceedings for being the inventor of a currency that was used in criminal activities. Or…don't move coins, lose all his funding and submit to a life of public embarrassment.

The argument for the former predicament being a legitimate concern seems to have stemmed from an article that appeared on a website called *Bitcoinist* on May 5th, with a headline that read "UK Law Enforcement Hint At Impending Craig Wright Arrest."

The threat that was fueling Wright's paranoia seemed real if more than a little fishy in its timing. The bigger issue, however, was that many thought the article had been written and submitted by Wright himself.

Whatever the truth actually was, Wright maintains he had no fear of criminal prosecution and therefore no reason to write such an article. "I'd already gone to the Australian government myself and told them everything about Bitcoin. We'd discussed it, had meetings. It was the public scrutiny that I didn't want. I didn't want it for me; I didn't want it for my family."

In any case, he chose to fall at the final hurdle, to snatch defeat from the jaws of potential victory. Wright had made his mind up that he would do no more to satisfy either the businessmen overlords or the world at large. As if to confirm it, a final blog post arrived on his website on May 5 that read:

> *"I believed that I could do this. I believed that I could put the years of anonymity and hiding behind me. But, as the events of this week unfolded and I prepared to publish the proof of access to the earliest keys, I broke. I do not have the courage. I cannot.*
>
> *When the rumors began, my qualifications and character were attacked. When those allegations were proven false, new allegations have already begun. I know now that I am not strong enough for this.*
>
> *I know that this weakness will cause great damage to those that have supported me, and particularly to Jon Matonis and Gavin Andresen. I can only hope that their honor and credibility is not irreparably tainted by my actions. They were not deceived, but I know that the world will never believe that now. I can only say I'm sorry. And goodbye."*

Craig Wright had chosen option two of those that were available to him: to lose all of his funding and to submit to a life of public embarrassment.

"I think he was part of a group, and it was somehow agreed that he would be the frontman for this outing," Andrew O'Hagan says. "They couldn't hold the line, or agree about proof, and from the minute I met him Craig was agonized about having to 'prove it.' He played it with me as if it was ridiculous ('What is proof anyway?') but he was tremendously upset about what MacGregor and co were asking of him. He said he needed the money, he'd got in deep, he wanted the backing for his other patents and such, but to my mind he was fronting a group who had been Satoshi, but neither the group nor he knew how to play it in the end."

Whatever Wright was, Robert MacGregor was in no mood to either unravel it or to reconcile. In the absence of the definitive proof that he'd tried so hard to engineer to make the Satoshi brand legitimate and commercially viable, he now had lost all belief. In his eyes, Wright had not only conned the world, but had also scammed his closest and only allies. "I mean—he's fucked me. Millions of dollars out of my pocket, nine months out of my life," MacGregor said to Andrew O'Hagan for his *London Review of Books* article.

Furthermore, rather than throwing good money after bad, Rob MacGregor was prepared to eat the large sum of cash he'd already sunk into the company that would later become nChain and send Craig Wright back to Australia with his tail between his legs to deal with his own problems.

"The day after all this, Rob MacGregor came to my office and sat down with me. He said, 'By the end of the day I want you to fire everybody that's working here and I want you to close this business down,'" Stefan Matthews recalls.

"I said, 'Rob, I can't do that. You're destroying the business and you're destroying an investment, just because you've got a bee up your arse about how things worked out.' He said, 'I'm giving you an instruction and I expect you to follow it,' and then he left."

MacGregor was out, and with him would go any future funding he'd guaranteed for the Satoshi project.

"I like and respect Rob a lot," Calvin Ayre says in reflection. "He is a brilliant lawyer and business person. Nothing Rob did was bad. In the right situation it could have been a brilliant strategy. However, his plan just did not properly consider Craig and this is how it all went sideways. I always was more inclined to do what Craig wanted to do, so was happy to be freed up to get directly involved in pursuing Craig's vision like I am now. Rob was critical in solving Craig's legal problems in Australia though, and enabling him to immigrate to the UK. Craig owes him thanks for this."

Meanwhile, faced with a terminal threat to the survival of a business that was barely beyond its infancy, Matthews started making phone calls.

"The first person I called was a financier friend of mine from Switzerland, Marco Bianchi," says Matthews. "I thought he was in Switzerland at the time but it turned out he was in Antigua. Not only that, he was sitting beside Calvin Ayre when his phone rang."

Matthews was calling Bianchi to tell him that the funding for the nChain was about to be cut off and that he was looking for potential ways by which to salvage the business.

"I've got Calvin sitting next to me. Let me put you on speaker," Bianchi said.

"What did you say to Rob?" Ayre asked Matthews.

Matthews explained how he'd been told to fire everyone and shutter the building.

"I'll talk to Marco now," Ayre said. "But under no circumstances should you act under those instructions."

"I'm not going to. If MacGregor wants to fire me, he can come and fucking do it himself," Matthews replied.

"You take care of what you need to do and look after the business that's been established. I'll talk to Rob. Either way, just know that we'll find a way to fix this," Ayre told him by way of reassurance.

After a tumultuous year where the best laid plans now lay in ruins, Bitcoin needed saving again.

CHAPTER **ELEVEN**

Regroup

One of the more overlooked aspects of the Bitcoin story is that despite the humiliation of Craig Wright's total capitulation in May of 2016 and the resultant departure of one of the main players behind the rescue package of 2015, the nChain business rolled forwards regardless, with Craig Wright still in place as its Chief Scientist.

Furthermore, the fact that few people in the Bitcoin world believed Wright was Satoshi Nakamoto after the confusing events of 2015 and 2016, didn't appear to matter very much. What was important was that Stefan Matthews and Calvin Ayre still believed.

"I don't think I screwed Rob MacGregor," Wright says in reflection. "In fact, I think he totally screwed me."

Wright's argument was that he should have never have had to prove anything with keys or coins in the first place.

"Everything they wanted me to do was the opposite of what I stood for. I have studied history and if you know the story of the Vikings, they got to shore and they burned the boats. To that extent, I knew that if I didn't burn the boats, there was one way forward as long as I had my keys," says Wright.

It seems certain that there was a fundamental disconnect between Wright's vision for the business and Robert MacGregor's.

Beyond that there was an even more fundamental disconnect between Robert MacGregor and Craig Wright the people. Wright wanted to build a business based on values over ten years or more, obviously with half an eye on making money in the process. MacGregor, Wright says, was only concerned in dollar value and cashing out quickly. The two men truly were, as Ayre had shrewdly identified previously, oil and water.

"When you care about more than the dollar value of something in this post-individualistic world, people just don't understand you," Wright reflects.

Throughout the remainder of 2016, what was formerly the nCrypt entity morphed into nChain with Robert MacGregor gone from the picture.

"Over the next six or seven months, Marco and I secured funding from a Maltese fund to buy out all of Rob MacGregor's shareholding interests," Stefan Matthews recalls.

In April of 2017, a press release went out to say that Malta-based Hi Tech Private Equity Fund SICAV plc. purchased nChain Holdings. An unknown source at the time claimed that $300 million would be invested in nChain over an undisclosed period and that the fund would be managed by the Lichtenstein-based Accuro Fund Solution, a part of the Zurich-based Accuro Group.

Waiting in the wings all the while was Calvin Ayre. Ayre had been observing the unsettling situation with the proof sessions from afar and providing advice from a distance where necessary.

"It didn't happen how I would have done it. I didn't really like the intermediary plan to sell the business, but because of my restrictions I kind of went along with it. At least then we'd have saved the technology," Ayre admits. "But once I became free of my longstanding legal constraints, we were able to get everything back on track as it was originally planned: me digging in and actually helping Craig prove that the technology works as he always said it did. I also so wanted to help him regain his legacy and intellectual property, both of which people had been trying to steal."

In July of 2017, Ayre's position did indeed change. The case against him was settled. He was now free to travel and to resume his international business career without fear of persecution by US authorities.

"Donald Trump actually did me a favor by winning the presidency," Ayre laughs. "He promoted Rod Rosenstein to Deputy Attorney General and he immediately got him into a scandal over James Comey because everything Trump touches gets scandalous. So, when Rosenstein left, he passed the file over to other people who just looked at it and said 'This isn't our file.' You don't get glory from taking over someone else's file so they just cut a deal with me and closed the file. That was the end of it. It was gone."

The timing couldn't have been better. When Calvin Ayre physically entered the Bitcoin world in 2017 to help Wright salvage both his invention and his legacy as the creator of it, his power and influence was certainly needed.

At the time, an era that has since become known as The Bitcoin Civil War was raging. Even though Craig Wright as Satoshi had returned, his control and influence had long gone, as had any respect the Bitcoin community had for him.

The scaling debate had only intensified after the formation of Blockstream in 2015. As Bitcoin's popularity increased, blocks (still limited to 1MB) filled up more quickly and transaction fees increased, ultimately reaching around five dollars. The big-block community to which Wright and Ayre belonged were still only focused on the utility potential of Bitcoin in the context of faster, cheaper transactions that could challenge industry behemoths like Visa and PayPal. The irony is that, prior to the formation of Blockstream in 2015, even some on the small-blocker side of the debate had acknowledged the potential benefits of increasing the block size limit. Unbelievably, Blockstream's co-founder Adam Back had once been in favor of raising block size limits in 2MB increments every two years to reach 8MB, as were other major players like Wladimir van der Laan, the primary Bitcoin Core code contributor, and renowned Bitcoin educator Andreas Antonopoulos.

But Blockstream had changed everything. By the end of 2015, the entire small-block community had gravitated toward Blockstream, and in doing so, the Bitcoin world had become more toxically divisive than at any previous time. Before long, big-block views were being censored left and right on Reddit forums like *Bitcoin Talk* controlled by small-block enforcers like Greg Maxwell who reportedly orchestrated an army of sock puppets to intimidate anyone with big-block opinions.

"Greg is either *the* super-villain or he's a major puppet stringpuller," Kurt Wuckert Jr. says, "He's famous for a pre-Bitcoin quote where he said, 'I have proven that distributed consensus was impossible,' which essentially was him saying that Bitcoin was impossible."

Maxwell's part in the Bitcoin story shouldn't be underestimated. A dreadfully smart man, according to those who have encountered him, Maxwell used his considerable talents as a software engineer and a social engineer having been friendly with the founders of Reddit and been involved in the early days of the Wikipedia foundation.

"Greg's role was apparently to come up with moderation policies." Wuckert Jr. explains, "He actually got removed from Wikipedia by his peers for the exact same thing he gets criticized for with Bitcoin: he was spinning up a bunch of fake accounts, he'd be having arguments with himself—crazy stuff like that. One of the policies he was accused of specifically violating was sock puppetry. He was accused of having all the qualities of a combatant terrorist in the way he pursued people with views he didn't agree with. It was the same with Bitcoin."

From 2016 onwards therefore, BTC was entirely controlled by Bitcoin Core developers like Greg Maxwell to conform to the Blockstream narrative.

Meanwhile, bitcoin mining nodes that didn't conform to Bitcoin Core's rules were subjected to DoS attacks that essentially froze big-block competitors such as Bitcoin XT (a fork created by developer Mike Hearn in 2014 with a view to increasing block size) and Bitcoin Classic (another soft fork of Bitcoin Core created in 2016 and supported by people like Gavin Andresen) out of the network altogether.

As if this wasn't bad enough, Blockstream were even developing their own decentralized (controlled by several entities rather than just one) payment protocol called the Lightning Network, which was aimed specifically at enabling fast, cheap transactions as a solution to the scaling debate. Any users who wanted to use BTC as a currency would then be forced to use Blockstream's proprietary Lightning Network "solution."

In layperson's terms, what all of this meant for Craig Wright in 2017 when his white knight Calvin Ayre rode over the horizon, was that—yes—he had invented Bitcoin and was back in the space. But he was back with a major problem to address. The bitcoin that existed in 2017 in no way resembled the vision Wright had had for electronic cash back in 2008. Not only that, he clearly felt that his intellectual property had essentially been hijacked and corrupted by Bitcoin Core developers who sought to lock him out and he had no obvious way of wresting it all back. Meanwhile, key figures in the Bitcoin world like Mike Hearn had become completely wearied by the toxicity of the community and walked away forever, in Hearn's case specifically citing Greg Maxwell's intransigence as one of the main reasons.

REGROUP

In his sign-off letter to the community, while referencing Bitcoin Core developers' stubborn approach to the scaling debate, Hearn wrote the following:

> *"One of them, Gregory Maxwell, had an unusual set of views: he once claimed he had mathematically proven Bitcoin was impossible. More problematically, he did not believe in Satoshi's original vision."*

The words *"Good luck, stay strong and I wish you the best,"* ended the letter.

"Ultimately, Mike Hearn would have stayed if it wasn't for Greg," Kurt Wuckert Jr. says. "And there are a lot of people with that same story."

When as reasonable a figure as Mike Hearn felt the need to walk away from Bitcoin, it became clear that something had to be done to regain some kind of control from Bitcoin Core developers and to re-establish Satoshi Nakamoto's position in the Bitcoin world. And the first step along that road came in July of 2017 with the development of the first hard fork in BTC to create Bitcoin Cash (BCH).

The best way to describe the creation of Bitcoin Cash on August 1st, 2017, would be as a big-blocker secession away from Bitcoin Core developers and small-blocker controlled BTC. The biggest takeaway of the split would be that where the BTC block size limit would remain at 1MB, BCH permitted block sizes of up to 8MB. To achieve this apostasy, a hard fork was created whereby the Bitcoin blockchain was duplicated and from there the two chains diverged forever, with each version's transactions recorded on separate ledgers thereafter.

Everyone who held BTC on August 1 was also given an equal amount of BCH. On that same day, in the face of catcalls saying that BCH proponents were simply creating money from thin air, BCH began trading at $240 while BTC sat at almost $2700. There was, however, method behind this radical move. BCH was intended as a contingency that came about in direct response to plans for something called SegWit (Segregated Witness), which itself was designed, in simplistic language for normal people, to allow protocol restrictions relating to block size to be bypassed.

The vision for SegWit actually dated back to an idea discussed between Greg Maxwell and fellow Bitcoin Core developers Peter Todd and Adam Back in 2013. Thereafter, it was developed into four proposals called BIPS (Bitcoin Improvement Proposals) by Bitcoin Core contributors Eric Lombrozo, Pieter Wullie, and Johnson Lau throughout 2015. To people like Craig Wright, SegWit was an affront to everything he'd ever created.

"I didn't see things like SegWit and Taproot coming," Wright admits, referencing a second update to the Bitcoin network that would take effect in 2021.

In his own blog, Wright identified threats to Bitcoin associated with SegWit being introduced:

> *"What is worse, this is an incentive for those wanting to destroy Bitcoin. attacking the existing network would be difficult and expensive. Any government or large organization seeking to attack Bitcoin could actually profit with the introduction of segregated witness."*

Elsewhere, he was more critical when he said, "*it's a boondoggle project by a group of developers with something to prove.*"

Although SegWit had not actually been implemented by the time BCH came to be, BCH was created pre-emptively in the event that SegWit would happen in the future. The big-blockers behind

BCH who opposed SegWit feared that the latter would lead to Bitcoin being viewed even more as an investment and not the peer-to-peer transactional entity it was intended to be. In time, they would be proved right.

One of the main players in the BCH movement was Roger Ver, a controversial figure in the technology world if ever there was one. Born in San Jose in 1979, Ver dropped out of high school to pursue business interests while carving out a rigid political identity as a libertarian and anarcho-capitalist. While running his own company, Memory Dealers; serving a brief prison sentence for sending large quantities of fireworks in the mail in 2002; and having moved to live in Japan in 2005, Ver first appeared on the Bitcoin scene in 2011 and was one of the five founders of the Bitcoin Foundation in 2012—a non-profit advocacy organization created ironically to restore Bitcoin's reputation in the aftermath of several scandals relating to online crime.

His first angel investment—$125,000—was into fellow Bitcoin Foundation founder Charlie Shrem's start-up company BitInstant, a service that allowed users to purchase items worldwide using bitcoin. With further sizeable investment from the Winklevoss brothers of Facebook infamy, BitInstant grew quickly and by 2013 was handling 30 percent of all Bitcoin transactions worldwide.

In 2014, the Bitcoin Foundation's own reputation took a severe knock when Shrem was sentenced to two years in prison for his involvement with Silk Road. BitInstant also closed down. Meanwhile, another of the foundation's founders, Mark Karpeles, would resign from the board on the back of his involvement with the Mt. Gox exchange scandal.

Although Ver would later declare his support for the incarcerated Silk Road founder Ross Ulbricht, he remained distant enough from the Silk Road wreckage to dodge trouble, and his best-known role was managing the cryptocurrency exchange and wallet developer Bitcoin.com between 2015 and 2019. Along the way he became known as "Bitcoin Jesus" because of his near evangelistic willingness to spread the word about the virtues of Bitcoin.

In 2017, as much as he was an advocate of libertarian and anarcho-capitalist views, Ver appeared to be a fan of increasing the block size limits required to make Bitcoin scale as Satoshi had intended. Indeed, in a 2017 interview with *Forbes*, Ver lamented where Bitcoin was going and conceded that the Bitcoin Core developers had negated Bitcoin's use as useable money / digital cash. To that extent, the views of Ver were undoubtedly aligned with the likes of Calvin Ayre and Craig Wright in 2017. All were united in their desire to increase block size and in turn facilitate people using bitcoin as a means to purchase goods and services while maintaining low transaction fees.

"The fact of the matter is, the utility of Bitcoin has been damaged," Ver told *Forbes*, referencing the software developer mind-set prevalent in BTC circles that was hamstringing its utility.

The launch of BCH was pre-dated by Craig Wright's sole public speaking appearance in 2017, which came at Arnhem, Holland on June 30th at a talk called Future of Bitcoin hosted by Jon Matonis, who by that stage had been appointed as nChain's Vice President of Corporate Strategy.

The event might as well have been billed *Satoshi: The Return (This Time It's Personal)*, so raw and impassioned was Wright's performance that day.

Having been introduced by Matonis as "Bitcoin Dundee," Wright strode onstage not in an Akubra hat with corks hanging from it, but in a pale blue dress shirt and stonewashed blue jeans. He then launched into arguably his most compelling manifesto ever about where he thought Bitcoin needed to go.

REGROUP

"Bitcoin can scale *right now*," Wright yelled. "I don't want a limit on demand. I want everyone on this globe to be using Bitcoin."

Clearly being propelled by a wave of high confidence, Wright, prowling the stage like a man possessed, continued to promote the stability of Bitcoin versus the instability of central banks.

"The problem is that central banks inflate. Who here actually knows what the Genesis block message was about? Who has read *The Times* page?" he asked a transfixed audience, while referencing the newspaper article name-checked in the Bitcoin Genesis block.

The thrust of Wright's incredible speech was that he was there for the long haul and determined to wrestle back control from the Core Developers who'd been damaging Bitcoin in his absence and stealing the security model.

"It's very simple," he said. "We'll help create and release code development that is not going to be taking from the core system. We will scale radically. And if you don't want to come along with us—stiff shit. It's very simple. I'm not going to be nice. You're with us, or you're against us."

If Craig Wright had been in any way damaged by the stressful events of 2016, it wasn't evident in his demeanor in Arnhem a year later. Instead, Wright looked fired up for the fight. Satoshi was reborn. In the context of the Bitcoin Civil War, it was his Gettysburg Address.

In early 2018, with Wright, Ayre, and Matthews in a holding position with the stopgap Bitcoin variant that was BCH, a hefty lawsuit landed on Craig Wright's desk.

Ira Kleiman, the brother of Wright's late friend Dave Kleiman, was suing Wright on behalf of the estate of his late brother, alleging Wright stole 1.1 million bitcoin and intellectual property related to Bitcoin from the partnership W&K Info Defense Research LLC, which had been set up in 2009, two years before the Tulip Trust was allegedly formed.

Highly significantly, the identity of who had invented Bitcoin was not actually being contested by Ira Kleiman when he filed the lawsuit in 2018. Indeed, the fact that Kleiman was bringing the lawsuit at all more or less confirmed that he knew Wright was Satoshi Nakamoto, the inventor of Bitcoin.

Instead, Kleiman's claim centered around the assertion that Wright, in his capacity as the inventor of Bitcoin, had millions of bitcoin and the associated IP over many years, and that his brother Dave was one half of that partnership. Ira Kleiman therefore believed that he was entitled to claim this 50 percent share, a share that he claimed Wright had stolen from The Tulip Trust after Dave Kleiman's death in 2013. It was further alleged that Wright had falsified and /or backdated documents to achieve this theft, and there were various estimates at the time as to how much was at stake. The range of assets being contested was somewhere between $10 billion and $25 billion dollars.

Wright, on the other hand, had a far less complicated stance. He simply flat-out denied that there was a partnership at all between him and Kleiman set up to mine bitcoin and develop valuable IP. This assertion of Wright's that Kleiman was both a good friend and occasional trusted collaborator but *not* a partner, was the point on which the entire lawsuit would rest.

From the outside, it was clear that the case was going to be complicated. For Ira Kleiman's part, his relationship with his late brother had not been particularly close and he hadn't preserved either documents or hard drives that might have helped him back up his claim, which instead relied on vague supposition. Indeed, he'd actually wiped hard drives and continued using them for other purposes. Disregard of this kind did not help his cause, nor did the fact that he didn't physically appear in court on the first day.

On Wright's side, access to definitive hard evidence was equally murky. The background to W&K, much like many of Wright's business entities, had always been confusing and with little reliable documentation to clarify how things were structured.

What was true, however, was that even before the case was heard, one important fact was undeniable: Dave Kleiman had died destitute in 2013 having defaulted on a mortgage and had even taken out a payday loan on the day of his death—all of this while making no attempt whatsoever to recover any of the 1.1 million bitcoin that his brother was now claiming he was entitled to. It just didn't add up—and it would all come out in court.

Court would have to wait, however. Because of the COVID-19 pandemic, the hearing that was scheduled to be heard in the US District Court for The Southern District of Florida, would ultimately be delayed until November 2021.

Meanwhile, at the front of the Bitcoin conflict, as much as BCH represented a continuation of Bitcoin's original protocol that had been threatened by changes like SegWit and Lightning Network, it was becoming clear that BCH's only USP was that it permitted block size increases to speed up transaction processing times. However, some, including Craig Wright and Calvin Ayre, argued that BCH didn't go far enough. In their view, any changes made to Bitcoin's protocol other than block size increases were deviations from that protocol and therefore not true to Satoshi Nakamoto's vision—a vision they wanted to completely reclaim and protect going forward. Although BCH seemed like an interim solution, that's all it was. It too continued to make changes to its protocol beyond what Satoshi purists deemed to be acceptable.

"In the past, Roger was supportive, but one of the reasons BCH split, apart from because they were arguing with me, was because they put in additions making it easier to do shady things," Craig

Wright explains. "They even had a blog post about it that I made them take down. I made sure to capture it though."

The blog post in question entitled "Taking OP_DATASIG out for a test drive" posted on Yours.Org by someone called Emil Oldenburg seemed to promote the use of what's called a bucket-shop contract. In a response to the blog on his own blog, Wright wrote at the time:

> "Roger Ver's Bitcoin.com representative recently posted a blog post detailing one of the many illegal and criminal use cases they plan to build into Bitcoin. The concept that a few (fools) seem to think adds value to Bitcoin is to alter the protocol to add the ability to create "permission-less" exchanges. What this means in simple terms is: Silk Road Version 2.0, Bucket Shops, Assassination markets, Money Laundering, for things like people smuggling and sex slavery."

Regardless of whether an underworld free-for-all was actually being implied by the proposed change in the BCH network upgrade (Wright himself replied in the blog's comments section suggesting the SEC would likely be interested), even the slightest suggestion of this kind of intention was never going to sit well with the Calvin Ayres and Craig Wrights of this world who sought to make Bitcoin both morally and physically transparent. The two sides of BCH's differing ideologies meant that something had to change.

In November of 2018, while Roger Ver and his side of BCH—Bitcoin Cash ABC—went off in one ideological direction taking the BCH ticker symbol with them, Craig Wright, Calvin Ayre, et al meanwhile went forward with Bitcoin Cash SV, which was soon rebranded to Bitcoin SV, and was assigned the ticker symbol BSV.

"Roger is a shareholder in some of the exchanges so he was able to get them to work with him to steal the BCH trading ticker for his new protocol," Calvin Ayre explains. "That forced us to get our own—BSV. He was trying to force Craig out of the sector and kill his life's work. In my opinion, he will do anything for money."

Finally, ten years after the white paper, Satoshi purists like Calvin Ayre, Stefan Matthews, and Bitcoin's creator Craig Wright had something to rally around that absolutely reflected the true and pure vision expressed in the white paper. Not only that, by creating BSV, they had taken the first major step down the road of recovering Wright's intellectual property from the clutches of Bitcoin Core developers.

One of the primary reasons for BSV's creation was that its development team believed that BCH's scalability features were unlikely to be enough to process the kind of transaction volumes that they thought Bitcoin would be capable of going forward. Furthermore, with the focus of BSV being on enterprise use of the Blockchain for business users and not store of value, BSV developers deemed it essential that their creation had the kind of built in stability that investors would certainly demand. As such, BSV was specifically designed to be both scalable and regulation-friendly in order to instill the kind of mainstream confidence that would lead to global enterprise adoption.

Restoring a version of Bitcoin that was true to Satoshi's 2008 vision was just one part of the aim for the BSV ecosystem that all of Calvin Ayre, Craig Wright, and Stefan Matthews were immersed in 2018. Beyond that there was a broader agenda: to push back against all those who claimed that any Bitcoin variant that wasn't BSV was not only fake Bitcoin, but also represented *theft* of Satoshi Nakamoto's intellectual property. As such, with BTC, BCH, and now BSV active in the arena and on the exchanges, the Bitcoin Civil War was far from won.

And war it certainly still was. The Bitcoin Core developers and indeed anyone else who did not want Satoshi Nakamoto's original protocol out there in the world and indeed whose business futures *relied* on their own alternative version of Bitcoin continuing, were not going to lie down without a fight.

"The many people who relied on Bitcoin as a means to commit anarchic acts had too much money on the line to quit. If I won, their dreams of dark money for committing dark acts would be ruined," Wright says.

As if BSV and Craig Wright didn't have enough opposition from Bitcoin Core supporters as it was, it also attracted the ire of previous allies like Roger Ver who, as much as he was a fan of block size increases conceptually, just couldn't get on board with any version of Bitcoin fronted by Craig Wright, who Ver viewed as a scammer and would say so publicly in a YouTube video where he announced "Craig Wright is a liar and a fraud, so sue me, again."

Although he'd been happy to support the initial BCH move, Ver's views on what Bitcoin should be had been made clear in a tweet a year earlier.

"Bitcoin was originally invented for crypto-anarchists, but has now become overrun by paternalistic autocrats," he tweeted.

"Roger is a deeply ideological anarcho-capitalist. It's politics first with Roger," Kurt Wuckert Jr. explains. "If you aren't on the anarchist team, he doesn't just disagree with you, he thinks of you the way others might think of a prison guard and Auschwitz."

It is unclear whether Ver's intense dislike for Wright was personal or ideological, however. Indeed, Ver, Wright, and Ayre had been photographed smiling together in a photograph taken in Japan in 2017 around the time of BCH's launch.

"Roger has told me in person more than once that he believes Craig is Satoshi," Ayre says. "Once was in Japan before they did their protocol fork and the other was at a dinner in Bangkok. Bit-coin kills all the crypto scams he is heavily invested in."

Whatever the reason, the net result remained the same: the BSV ecosystem had acquired one more influential enemy by the end of 2018.

"I tried to be nice; everyone wanted me to work with him but that was never going to work. I used to help the police take down child porn rings and people like Roger seem to want to make things like that easier for people like that because of his anti-government / anti-law stance," Wright says. "He tries to say he just sold fire-works, but what he actually sold were explosives."

CHAPTER **TWELVE**

Fight Back

Having restored Bitcoin to what they saw as Satoshi's original protocol, the men behind Bitcoin SV set about setting up a support mechanism to counter dissenting voices which by this point had, in the case of Bitcoin Talk on Reddit, actually booted big-blocker users off their forum altogether to leave themselves with what amounted to a toxic BTC echo-chamber where the agonized voices of trolls howled into the void day and night.

Calvin Ayre's answer was to adapt *CoinGeek* from being the Bitcoin utility coverage site it had been since 2015 into an even flashier online presence for all things Bitcoin SV and beyond. From there it would refashion further into being a multi-media organization that hosted events and conferences worldwide to promote the real Bitcoin and the utility potential of the Blockchain in general. Simultaneously, Ayre, Matthews, and Wright founded the official body to promote all things BSV—the Zurich-based Bitcoin Association for BSV. Ayre's vision was to create a new industry where BSV could be used not only for micro-transactions but also in the world of supply chain and data management.

All of this was done against a backdrop of enduring conflict in the wider Bitcoin world. Small blockers in the BTC space that had invested their reputations and livelihoods on the notion that

Bitcoin couldn't adequately scale and would "break" if it did, were now confronted with a version of Bitcoin founded on Satoshi's protocol where block sizes of 100MB and much more were possible with nothing breaking.

"Adam Back once told me that the white paper was wrong and that Bitcoin wasn't really about micro-payments anymore," says Craig Wright. "He said the community had moved on from that and my comment was that I never even mentioned the word community at any point. If the community of Apple decides that they don't like Apple they can move on to Samsung, but they don't get to rename Apple. This community idea is just communist shit."

For a so-called community entrenched in the idea that a 1MB block size limit was the ceiling, the reality that BSV could handle very large block sizes and remain stable was hard to take. While the BTC crew were being paid to talk at conferences to assert that their fake version of Bitcoin was simply a store of value, Craig Wright was out there telling the world that the real Bitcoin had zero limits.

Inevitably, instead of just attacking Wright's restored Bitcoin, BTC devotees inevitably turned their focus on Wright himself. He was heckled, jeered, abused online, and had death threats sent to his family. It was a siege at times, but he never broke. Instead, Wright, invigorated by the act of seizing back control had decided there was to be no more Mr. Nice Guy.

"I tried to be nice," Wright explains. "But it doesn't fucking work. People just take it in the wrong, and it gets me nowhere. I decided I wasn't going to budge on anything ever again. They can try to silence me all they want, but it'll end up in court."

Small-blocker attacks weren't just limited to Wright. With Calvin Ayre now prominent in the Bitcoin world, no invitation was needed to go after him on the basis of his opulent lifestyle and his lengthy cold war with the US authorities.

The logic used by the trolls was that, if Ayre had committed some kind of indiscretion in the past then surely he had to be committing another by backing Wright. Of course, this "logic" made no sense at all. Few bothered to look into the small print of Ayre's issues with the US to establish that Ayre was actually the victim. For them, the fact that he'd had a public run-in with US authorities at all was sufficient reason to doubt his credentials and to tar him with the same negative brush as Wright.

"People tried to make out that Calvin was some kind of terrorist but people forget that they took millions of dollars of his money," Wright says. "I'd seen stunts like this before. When I worked at Sporting Bet I was in the office one day when everyone stopped and started looking at the TV. It turned out that the Sporting Bet CEO had been arrested when he landed in America. They kept him for two days while they made a fuss about it and then he went back to the UK. The US love to shake innocent people down."

For Calvin Ayre the ad-hominem attacks were like water off a duck's back.

"I pay no attention. Twitter isn't the real world," Ayre says. "I'm focused on developing real business solutions with Bitcoin and protecting Craig's legacy. The trolls aren't important. I can silence them with facts. Bitcoin ends their scams."

Where Ayre was happy to combat dissenting voices on Twitter, Stefan Matthews was happier to remain in the background devising strategy for nChain and beyond.

"I didn't deliberately shy away from public appearances, but I didn't seek them out either. I'm a private person by nature," Matthews says.

Matthews had better things to do. One of his main areas of focus was bitcoin mining, a logical complement business to sit alongside Bitcoin BSV.

"I created and built BMG, a mining operation, originally part of the NCH group. Then I created and built a private mining operation for Calvin," Matthews explains. "Overlapping this were the investments Calvin and I made in Squire Mining which we took control of and rebranded and expanded as TAAL."

TAAL, founded in 2019, describes its own purpose as "Facilitating businesses building applications and contributing data onto a public, permission-less and scalable blockchain." With TAAL in place and the BSV Genesis upgrade completed in January of 2020, the future for true Bitcoin looked bright. According to the Bitcoin SV's own website, the upgrade was the last piece required to restore Bitcoin to what it had been at the time of Satoshi's white paper in 2008:

> "The Genesis upgrade restored the original Bitcoin Protocol as closely as possible to Satoshi's original design, locking it down to create stability for developers and enterprises to build upon. Unbounded scaling returned, as did the original Bitcoin script language that allows developers to build on-chain applications easier."

Another significant date arrived in January 2020 when Craig Wright, having been subjected to multiple court orders from lawyers representing Ira Kleiman compelling him to disclose information about the Tulip Trust, was rumored to be soon to receive the missing information that he claimed had prevented him from accessing this trust since it had been set up in 2011. In a statement, Wright said the following:

> "As I've explained in court proceedings, I believe I will receive information in January 2020 that will enable us to identify coins I mined into my compa-

nies in 2009 and 2010, but cannot be certain that all of that information will in fact arrive. I have not said the private keys to those coins would become available, or if so, actually used, in January 2020. In the next few weeks, we will be holding trust meetings and working out the next steps going forward in 2020."

In a story that felt like it had been plucked straight from a James Bond script, a "bonded courier" was said to be arriving in January to deliver to Wright keys to a registry that would unlock the trust that apparently held in the region of 1.1 million BTC, which, at that particular moment, would have been worth in the region of $8000 each.

As much as the suggestion of a bonded courier conjured images of a leather clad motorcycle outrider with a package handcuffed to his or her person, or even an armored truck rolling across London to Craig Wright's house, nobody really knew how, exactly, this delivery would happen.

"I've heard from people that would know that the bonded courier wasn't an actual person but just a time-lock application in the Bitcoin script," Kurt Wuckert Jr. says. "You can program a smart-contract so that coins aren't accessible until a specific day."

Regardless of what or who the bonded courier was, something indeed happened. Wright's attorneys duly notified the court that they had provided "the necessary information and key slice to unlock the encrypted file." This inevitably led to speculation that Wright genuinely had had to wait until January 2020 for this information and that he hadn't simply been stalling.

The possibility that Wright might receive this vast fortune of BTC was incredible enough. The suggestion that he might even sell them and in the process tank the BTC market sent shockwaves of panic through the Bitcoin community as the BTC price sat at

$8500. Wright, however, was quick to dismiss these rumors in a statement that read:

> *"I do not intend to dump my family's BTC as some people suspect or want, as this would hurt many people in the industry. Instead, I will work with the family trust to implement plans to slowly move the interests of the trust into a sustainable model that builds the Bitcoin SV environment and ensures that the Bitcoin that I originally envisioned more than a decade ago (now known as Bitcoin SV—BSV) continues to grow strongly."*

The implications of the "bonded courier" story were important in the context of the approaching Kleiman trial, which was scheduled for November 2021. Not only would it absolve Wright of accusations that he'd been trying to deceive the court, but it would also prove, once again, that he was Satoshi Nakamoto. Why else would someone have access to a trust for bitcoins they mined between 2009 and 2011 if that person hadn't actually mined them and could also produce signed documents to show that they'd created the trust?

"Part of me thinks the whole trusts thing is a lie because why wouldn't it be?" Kurt Wuckert Jr. says. "If somebody asked me where I've got my trillion dollars hidden, I'm going to have a pretty good story. I would want people to think I'm crazy to throw them off the scent. So it could be that, but I also just tend to think that Craig just has the keys and a shit ton of Bitcoin from real early and I kind of think that the Tulip Trust might be all bullshit. I think it's smoke and mirrors and he has the keys."

Just a couple of weeks after the bonded courier saga, and presumably timed to coincide with the date Wright would regain access to the mysterious Tulip Trust, the publication of the book about Wright entitled *Behind the Mask: Craig Wright and the Battle for Bitcoin*, suddenly didn't happen. However, just one week before it was due to hit bookstore shelves, somebody somewhere hit the brakes.

The publisher, a small Melbourne based outfit called Affirm Press were approached for comment by *CoinGeek*. All they said in response was: "We have postponed the publication of this book indefinitely."

Nothing more has been said about the title in the three years since its original January 28, 2020 publication date.

Several theories swirled about what had happened with a book that had reputedly generated quite significant pre-order interest on the back of an intriguing promo description that read:

> *"Blackmail, police raids, hidden fortunes, death threats and a billion dollar offshore trust. This is the thrilling, stranger-than-fiction story of Craig Wright, the Australian who controversially claims to be the real Satoshi Nakamoto, the elusive inventor of Bitcoin and the underpinning technology that is proving as disruptive as the web was 25 years ago. Behind the Mask spans continents and features a cast of characters ranging from a libertarian femme fatale to a fugitive Canadian gambling tycoon. It follows Wright from his humble beginnings in dirt-poor Queensland to be-suited guru trying to recover his reputation and control over the cryptocurrency stage, squaring up to multiple enemies."*

The book was highly anticipated, and understandably so, given the tone of the promised content. Two weeks before release, Calvin

Ayre tweeted an Amazon link to the book along with a tweet that read: "*This is coming fast and will cement Craig as Satoshi to mainstream business media.*"

The two journalists involved responsible for researching and co-writing the book—Reuters's Jeremy Wagstaff and Byron Kaye— were both experienced in the technology world and more than qualified to tell the story. Neither commented publicly when the book wasn't published.

"I know someone bought it out and squashed it but it certainly wasn't our side of things—people even claimed it was me who did," says Wright. "I liked those guys and had spoken to them from time to time and met them at conferences for a coffee and such. I didn't talk to them a lot for that book but they seemed to have good intentions. They cared more about the truth than anything else. Their angle was that I was Satoshi."

"I had some discussions with those guys at Reuters," Wright's former accountant John Chesher says. "The writers were trying to be real honest and forthright. They were two good guys just trying to find out what the hell was going on. I talked to them a bit, pointed them in a few directions at times—nothing untoward that would have damaged anyone. There was a lot of fuss when their book was ready to get published and that was when some shutdown activity went on. I can't say this with any validity, but I always had a sense that it was their own employer, Reuters, who shut that book down."

Whatever the precise reasons for shutting down what seemed like a well-intended book about Wright's involvement with the invention of Bitcoin, that's exactly what happened, and Calvin Ayre for one wasn't happy about it, tweeting: "*Core/BTC gang has blocked this to stop the truth about Bitcoin coming out. Craig was supporting and cooperating with the authors of this book so this is FUD to say its fear of him that caused this. These criminals will do anything to keep this quiet. I will publish this.*"

"There are so many people that don't want me to be Satoshi because I'm anti all that anarchist bullshit. Shutting down one book in Australia doesn't silence me though," Wright says. "I won't go away."

As if 2020 hadn't started intriguingly enough, Craig Wright then suffered a substantial hack, which he discovered on February 8. Coins belonging to an entity called Tulip Trading Ltd. were said to be controlled by keys stored on Wright's computer at his home in Surrey. Wright noticed three outgoing transactions, two very large, from a Bitcoin wallet he held. After further investigation, he also discovered that files containing multiple white papers and associated research data had been wiped from cloud storage—in addition to his means to access a vast amount of holdings held at other wallet addresses. The implications were huge.

To the outsider, the timing of the hack might have seemed a little suspect. One month after receiving the means to access a trust that he hadn't been able to get into for over a decade containing vast amounts of BTC, and Wright then gets hacked? For some, that all seemed a little too convenient.

Wright maintained at the time that he had no idea how the hack occurred. His only theory, and even this seemed far-fetched, was that it had happened because of a random wireless router he subsequently found in his house that nobody recognized.

"I believe that it must have been planted there by the hackers, either when tradesmen were in our home or by breaking in. This is being considered by the police and me in the context of the ongoing investigation," Wright's statement at the time said.

After the hack, Wright apparently wiped the hard drives of the computers in question in case any malware remained.

"My computer contained a great deal of confidential information. I wiped my hard drive in order to ensure all possible threats were removed from my network and it was simply not practicable to take a copy of any of these drives," Wright explains.

Predictably, Wright detractors were quick to claim that the hack didn't take place at all and that Wright was simply orchestrating yet another of his complicated scams. Even the fact that Wright had reported the hack to the police as soon as he uncovered it and had both a crime reference number and the name of the investigating officer, wasn't enough. Many still believed that Wright had invented the hack for reasons only he knew, knowing that it would be difficult to disprove.

"I also note the irony that I am being accused of 'inventing' a hack. That is precisely what the then BTC developers did when they removed Gavin Andresen's site access right after he acknowledged me as Satoshi," Wright said, referencing that fact that when Gavin Andresen repeated his endorsement of Wright as Satoshi in New York in 2016, the anti-Craig Wright community falsely claimed that Andresen's earlier blog post was not actually written by him.

As for the identity of Wright's hackers, that is still unknown. However, since the hack, Wright, as part of his offensive against BTC developers, initiated a legal debate over property rights as far as they relate to Bitcoin. As a result, Wright's lawyers initially sent letters to BTC developers Wladimir van der Laan, Jonas Schnelli, and Pieter Wullie and referred to the hack in February of 2020. Although the developers were not themselves accused of conducting the hack, Wright's argument instead focused on his belief that the coins were still the property of Tulip Trading Ltd. and therefore those developers had a legal responsibility to ensure no illegitimate transactions took place with the coins. The letters also restated Wright's claim to the Satoshi Nakamoto pseudonym and asserted that Tulip Trading Ltd. owns the right to the name Bitcoin and the Bitcoin database. The latter point reinforced a previous claim by

Wright that said: as the original creator of Bitcoin he is the rightful owner of the name and database, and any other software utilizing these concepts must cease doing so, or pay a licensing fee.

As much as the letters were initially treated with disdain by the BTC side of the argument, the action was indicative of Wright's stance on defending his intellectual property, and if necessary, going to court to enforce it. As such, some developers, including the first mentioned van der Laan, have since resigned. Other resignations would follow. Wright's stance had clearly instilled fear.

In simple terms, Tulip Trading was seeking to have developers recognized as "fiduciaries" with legal obligations to users. If the developers were to lose in court, there's a possibility that they could be forced to write software patches to help recover Tulip Trading's Bitcoin (in 2023 the claim against fifteen developers was granted permission to go to trial).

Speaking of court, Kleiman v Wright eventually came around in November of 2021 and was an opportunity for Craig Wright to wheel out some big guns in the context of proving to the world that he was Satoshi Nakamoto. Although this truth wasn't actually questioned in the lawsuit itself, Wright and his lawyers nevertheless used the trial to overwhelm not only Ira Kleiman, but the wider world as well.

Wright introduced a whole host of witnesses, all of them highly credible and who were able to describe historical interactions dating back many years that proved beyond doubt that Wright had invented Bitcoin in 2008, following many years of experimentation in other industries such as banking, gambling, telecommunications, and the Australian Stock Exchange.

One of the more fascinating testimonies came from Wright's uncle Don Lynam, a former RAAF wingman and a man of unimpeachable integrity and standing. Lynam described his relationship with Wright and also Wright's close relationship with his grandfather. Much more significantly, Lynam described how Wright had shown him early iterations of the white paper. Even though the paper Lynam saw didn't actually contain the word Bitcoin, Lynam was certain enough to state under oath that he was sure the paper was referencing it. Lynam then went on to describe how he physically ran one of the first Bitcoin nodes on his computer at home shortly after it was launched in 2009.

Equally compelling was the re-appearance of Gavin Andresen, who'd been deposed to bring his recollections of his interactions with Wright in front of the court via video link. While clearly nervous about appearing in such a high-profile case, Andresen responded cautiously but said nothing to retract his previously stated belief that Craig Wright was indeed Satoshi Nakamoto. Indeed Andresen confirmed, again that Wright had signed several early blocks with Satoshi keys. While he acknowledged that he, like most people, had been a little confused ("bamboozled," to quote him directly) by Wright's blog post on May 2, 2016, Andresen stated to the court that he still believed he was Satoshi Nakamoto, the inventor of Bitcoin.

Finally, there were written notes from Allan Granger, Wright's former colleague at BDO. These notes clearly showed Wright discussing with him a peer-to-peer cash system prior to the release of Bitcoin.

Game over? Not quite.

For all the positives that came out of the Kleiman trial, it wasn't by any means perfect for Wright. The lawyers for the plaintiff leaned heavily into the idea that multiple examples of documentation they'd been presented with had been manipulated or forged.

"There was a ton of that stuff," says Kurt Wuckert Jr. "But I think that if Craig was Satoshi and disappeared for good in 2011, he would have done everything in his power to destroy every bit of evidence that he was Satoshi. He would have to have done. He's a ninja of forensics but he's really bad at faking documents. But because of this position he found himself in, where the game had shifted, maybe he tried to recreate his evidence and did a really bad job."

For Wright's part, he always seemed to have an answer, and the answer usually involved the same dismissive suggestions that no doubt tied up the opposition lawyers in mental knots: that other people were involved, he was hacked and that the documents in question had been manipulated to frame him so that Ira Kleiman could insert himself into a story he hadn't ever been involved with, for his own financial gain. After all, lengthy due diligence had been done. As such, Ira Kleiman surely would not have proceeded with such a costly exercise if he didn't think there was a possible payoff at the end of it.

"There was a moment at the trial where I realized it was Ira Kleiman all along who'd been scheming with the ATO and the *WIRED* and *Gizmodo* journalists to frame me," Wright explains. "Finally, everything made sense, but it took six years for me to discover it for sure."

"When I was in Miami at the trial, something kind of leaked," Kurt Wuckert Jr. recalls. "When Ira was on the stand answering questions saying something like, 'well, when I was talking with the magazines...' I saw Craig throw his hands up in the air as if to say, 'It was you, you son of a bitch!' When we went out for lunch, Craig grabbed me by my jacket and said, 'It was fucking Ira!'"

While the Kleiman trial didn't answer every question regarding Wright's involvement with Bitcoin, it certainly took care of a few—the main one being that Wright had no partnership with Dave Kleiman regarding Bitcoin holdings and therefore couldn't have stolen from him. Beyond that, the trial also established that

Wright most likely did have access to substantial holdings of Bitcoin, perhaps even the one million plus that was rumored.

The plaintiff's attempt to challenge this by bringing in Jamie Wilson, Wright's former CFO for two years, essentially backfired when Wilson reluctantly concluded that Wright did indeed have huge quantities of bitcoin and he couldn't say beyond doubt that Wright's bitcoin had come from any other source than by being mined by Wright himself. Wilson's testimony added even more detail to the period where Wright's life seemed to be most traumatic. Wilson, a tech guy himself, had met Wright sometime in 2012 as he was looking for help to get his business, a company called Cryptoloc, off the ground in the aftermath of losing everything, he claimed, in the devastating Queensland floods of 2010.

"Jamie didn't lose anything during the flooding," Wright says. "He lived in an area that was miles away from anywhere that was flooded, at least 20km."

Regardless, Wright and Wilson seemingly got along and Wright not only helped Wilson, but he also ended up hiring him as CFO of a couple of his companies during 2013. Where this story gets strange is that, as much as Wilson claimed to be CFO, he also testified that he didn't actually have access to the accounts of the companies that he was meant to be overseeing.

"So, although I had the title of the CFO, my capacity as an accountant, I was not given full control, nor did I even have access to zero [sic]," Wilson told the trial via video.

Even though Wilson was shown various emails in which he was cc'd around this period in 2013—emails between Craig Wright and the Australian Tax Office that discussed millions of dollars—Wilson still claimed to be in the dark.

For casual observers, Jamie Wilson's testimony made no sense. If he was brought there to damage Wright's reputation, it looked as if his presence was achieving the opposite.

And it was personal.

In his testimony, Wilson claimed that, during 2013, Craig Wright's dress sense changed and that he went from being a hoodie and jeans wearing tech geek to wearing fancy suits and watches. Wilson also expressed dismay at how much Wright spent on a particular staff party. All of Wilson's claims pointed to him being little more than a disgruntled employee who was jealous about his boss's success at a time when bitcoin's price was approaching its highest peak to date of close to $1000.

In his deposition, Wright had his own theories. Wright had never been shy to say that staff had always liked to take advantage of him. He had also claimed that some members of staff had tried to steal his IP and sell it as their own. In his deposition, Wright singled Jamie Wilson out specifically in this regard.

"Jamie Wilson was working with a person that I fired and also Jamie Wilson has fabricated a number of documents, such as power of attorney over the patent that I created," Wright said.

Who knows what the relationship between Wilson was really like, but Wright's claim, in combination with Wilson's confusing testimony, certainly lends weight to the possibility that, as he has said all along, Craig Wright's staff were indeed colluding against him. When you add the fact that Wilson apparently made a point of directly contacting Ira Kleiman's lawyers to congratulate them for going after his former boss when he first heard about the case in 2018, it's easy to reach the conclusion that Wilson was perhaps a jealous employee turned anti-Wright witness in the context of the Kleiman trial.

In summary, the Kleiman trial benefitted Craig Wright more than it didn't. By being given the opportunity to bring in some highly convincing witnesses that had never been previously heard from, Wright undoubtedly enhanced his reputation considerably in an extremely high-profile trial that attracted a lot of mainstream press attention.

"Ira was just stupid," Wright says. "He was only out for money. He thought that if he could bankrupt me, he'd benefit. But it was the opposite: if he'd bankrupted me he'd have got nothing. I made offers to him after Dave's death that he should have taken. But he was greedy, and because of that he got nothing. He simply tried to insert himself into the story for money. He gave falsified information to the ATO with a view to fabricating a huge lawsuit. And he used a different email every time when sending information to the magazines and the tax office. Nobody talks about that."

"The Kleiman trial lifted any remaining cloud of suspicion from Craig Wright," Calvin Ayre says. "We will now see investors wanting to partner with us. It's a win."

In the middle of 2022, I contacted Craig Wright and asked if we could talk. A few things were bothering me, and I needed some answers.

As I spoke to people about the story, I started noticing a few themes. Certain parts of the story people were fine with talking about; others got shut down completely with no explanation. When that happens often enough, you start wondering why.

One of such subjects on my list to discuss was the two personalities that are Joseph Vaughn Perling and Uyen Nguyen. One source I'd spoken to said, "A bit of friendly advice: leave this alone." Another claimed that Vaughn Perling and Nguyen were married and that the former had much more to do with the beginnings of Bitcoin than anybody knew. Yet another said both Vaughn Perling and Nguyen were "unfindable" and for specific reasons. And yet another claimed that Nguyen "needed to be protected."

In the absence of any contact with either of them, and believe me I tried, I'd hit a brick wall. If there was something sinister going on, I didn't particularly expect Wright to tell me. I suppose I just wanted to hear and see what he said. I called him on Zoom at the agreed time and there he was, wearing large headphones. He was friendly and relaxed and seemed happy to talk.

"What's the story with Uyen?" I asked. "I keep getting shut down whenever I ask anyone."

"There isn't really anything to say," Wright said, "She's, let's see, now twenty-something, can be a bit…unrelenting."

"That's it? So, why would anyone say that she needed protection?"

"She's strange in some ways," Wright said.

"But she held keys. Is there a legal threat to her?"

"She was never a trustee. I had multiple things and she held certain key slices to certain things," he said.

"Does she still hold key slices?"

"I have no idea. I couldn't tell you."

If I was looking for clarity on the Uyen Nguyen, I was getting precisely the opposite. Wright was visible on a screen that was ten inches away and was talking, but he might as well have been on another planet. I still felt there was something he just wasn't telling me and had no intention of doing so.

"What about Joseph?"

"Well, Joseph was around the Bitcoin scene forever, since ancient history," he told me. "He was also involved with the Ian Grigg types at one time."

"Okay, but was Joseph involved directly in the invention of Bitcoin? I'm asking you this very directly as I need to know."

Wright paused. "No, no. I mean he did a whole lot of things on his own…the normal stuff. He got in trouble for what he was doing at one stage…"

"Are we talking about New Liberty Dollar here?" I cut in.

"Yes, we are. But lots of people did."

"So there's no sinister backdrop here that I'm not being told?"

"No, nothing like that. It's just that…Uyen can be emotional."

"Do you know where she is?"

"Not really," Wright said (which I didn't believe), "but she's married with a child. Other than that, I don't really know."

"And she has no involvement with Bitcoin whatsoever nowadays?"

"If she's doing something with Joseph, I don't know," he said.

"So she and Joseph are together?" I asked.

"I'm not sure," Wright replied.

It wasn't going anywhere, but it was clear that my pushing wasn't going to change anything. I left it.

A few people along the way had told me that Wright had been embroiled in some kind of scandal in 2013 relating to gold, gold mining and a convicted Australian criminal by the name of Michael Ferrier. John Chesher, Wright's accountant, had alluded to problems, but hadn't really spelled the nature of them out.

It seems that while Wright was trying to get his Bitcoin Bank off the ground, he thought it would be a good idea to back it with gold. Why the inventor of Bitcoin would need to back a venture with gold, I had no idea. And there were mixed reports online about what had actually gone down.

"What's the story with Michael Ferrier?" I asked Wright directly.

"Ha, well. I needed to actually have gold to make a backed system," Wright said. "And I was dumb enough to think that I'd get more value if I had something ongoing. When Ferrier first started, he had a real business plan. He wasn't out there conning everyone at the beginning. The problem was, like many mining situations, the deals weren't coming through fast enough and he didn't have enough money. Eventually, he couldn't pay the bills. Rather than begging or going bankrupt, he lied and said there was much more gold than there actually was."

"What did you want from him?" I asked. "Your accountant said you wanted banking technology?"

"Well, no. He introduced me to people he knew because he was dealing with Arabs who were associated with a Saudi bank. Fortunately, I'd designed Bitcoin to be Halal and not Haram. I'd studied Arabic finance to make sure it all aligned because I thought it would be a good selling point. I thought that if I could get banking software and then modify it to handle everything, then off I went."

"And did you?"

"I got the damn software, but I never got the bank launched. I was in the process of getting a banking license and all the rest but in the aftermath of Silk Road, everything got shut down. They painted me with the same brush. Everyone said 'Oh, what you're doing is for crime.'"

"Did you have to pay Ferrier?"

"I'd already paid him for some of the software, but I assumed that the gold would also come through. It didn't, and I got conned."

Wright's explanation seemed as plausible a version as I was ever likely to get. I wondered if my next area of enquiry would yield similarly satisfactory results.

"Once and for all, how many coins are left in the Seychelles Trust?" I asked.

"Well, it's actually the Tulip Trust," Wright said, "and none. What I keep trying to explain to people is that the trust owns corporations. So, the corporations own coins. For example, Tulip Trading owns around 110,000 that I'm about to go through court to get back. They got stolen because everybody knows who the fuck I am. The other companies, Wright International Investments formed in August 2009 because the ATO was causing me problems in Australia, which was a good move at the time."

"Nobody talks about Wright International Investments though," I said.

"Nobody even knew about it, so nobody tried to fabricate false documents about it!" Wright said. "They'll have a hard time anyway because I used MYOB in Australia, a cloud-based accounting platform, and the logs date back to 2009. The lawyers have them all. How do I prove it? Well, it was August 2009 and it showed I owned all the Satoshi coins. If I'm not Satoshi, wouldn't that be a stupid thing to do?"

The final area I wanted to quiz Wright on was perhaps the one thing that instilled more doubt in his detractors than anything else: forged / false documents. But first, some background.

Wright had been involved in two trials in 2022, one in the UK where he was embroiled with the YouTube personality Peter McCormack and the other in Norway with "Hodlonaut," a Norwegian school teacher whose real name was Magnus Granath.

In May 2022, Wright and Peter McCormack finally squared off in court with the latter accused of defaming Wright by calling him a fraud in relation to his claim to be Satoshi Nakamoto, the inventor of Bitcoin. The case had been rumbling on in the background for almost three years after a series of 2019 tweets by McCormack claiming Wright was a fraud.

"Craig Wright is not Satohis [sic]!" he wrote. "When do I get sued?"

The answer wasn't long in coming when Wright sued for libel in August of 2019. In the three years after the lawsuit was issued, McCormack's position changed from one where he was no longer claiming Wright wasn't Satoshi, but merely that his defaming of Wright by saying such hadn't caused material damage. Some speculated that there was a specific reason for this: that McCormack and his legal team had seen enough in the pre-trial discovery process to make the assessment that to dispute Wright's Satoshi status would be a losing battle. Instead, they settled for a lesser charge, and in layperson's terms, hoped to get away leniently.

The end result was that Wright proved his case for defamation, albeit that he was accused of presenting false evidence (withdrawn before trial) stating that because of the defamation campaign, he had been disinvited from a number of speaking engagements worldwide. Although this evidence technically wasn't presented and was found not to be true, the judge took a dim view of what he saw as Wright's underhand attempt and he was awarded just £1 for his troubles. However, the monetary aspect of the case was never the point. Wright was using the power of the court to rehabilitate his reputation.

The Hodlonaut trial was a slightly different situation. Hodlonaut too had tweeted claiming Wright was a fraud, "mentally ill," and a scammer in 2019. However, the case wasn't specifically about defamation, but about whether Hodlonaut's actions were protected by Norway's freedom of speech laws. At the time, Wright had asked for the tweets to be removed, and they were. But Wright also asked that Hodlonaut release a statement saying that Wright was Satoshi Nakamoto. This statement was not forthcoming and so the case ended up in court in September 2022.

If Kleiman v Wright was an opportunity for Wright to wheel out the heavy artillery to defend his Satoshi Nakamoto claims, the trial in Norway facilitated the mobilization of lethal nukes.

"It was incredible to witness the contrast between each side. On Hodlonaut's side, there was endless metadata that even seemed to confuse the judge. On Craig's side, it was just a procession of professional, assured witnesses," Kurt Wuckert Jr. recalls.

Each witness appeared and presented compelling, calm evidence that reinforced Wright's claim to be Satoshi Nakamoto. The court heard from Stefan Matthews, who told the story of their early interactions at BDO and his first sighting of the white paper in 2008. Robert Jenkins, who Wright had met in the late '90s while working for Vodafone, showed up and serenely presented Craig Wright as a model professional with whom he later discussed digital currency. Then there was Shaoaib Yusuf, a Dubai-based businessman who'd met Wright in Australia in 2006, talked to him about blockchain and even visited his farm in rural New South Wales and saw Wright's racks of hardware with his own eyes…

As if the Hodlonaut side of the courtroom's heads weren't spinning enough at the avalanche of evidence raining down open them, Wright then brought in Neville Sinclair, who worked with Wright at BDO in 2007 and who confirmed the conversation Wright had claimed he had with his boss Allan Granger.

Behind Sinclair came Wright's nephew Max Lynam who, after describing how much time he spent with Wright when they were children and confirmed Wright's close relationship with his genius grandfather, went on to explain how Wright had asked the family to run software in their home which they were later informed might have accrued quite significant money for them.

Although Lynam's testimony didn't go as far as to say he knew Wright was Satoshi Nakamoto, he said enough to indicate, beyond reasonable doubt, that Bitcoin was what Wright was likely working on in 2008 and beyond. "We weren't surprised to hear he was Satoshi," Lynam said, when questioned on the stand.

Finally, there was David Bridges, a former employee of Qudos Bank in Australia, who'd also met Craig. He described, much like Neville Sinclair had, how Wright tried to pitch him what was essentially Bitcoin in the year or two prior to 2008.

In response to many of these calm testimonies by people of professional standing over many years with no reason other than a wish to tell the truth to put their entire reputations on the line, there were very few questions from the Hodlonaut side.

"What could they say?" Kurt Wuckert Jr. says. "Asking questions would have only have made their positions worse. More information would only have made Craig's Satoshi claims stronger."

That Wright lost the Hodlonaut case was immaterial. Norway's free speech laws are different from other countries and a parallel case is set for the UK court in 2023—in addition to an appeal of the Norway case set to be heard in front of three senior judges. For all the technicalities, and the freedom of speech aspect was just that, the trial in Norway represented one more step down the road of Craig Wright proving once and for all that he is Satoshi Nakamoto, the inventor of Bitcoin.

With just one caveat…

The false and forged documents accusations came up again at the Hodlonaut trial and for anyone not in Wright's corner, it is always going to be a nagging doubt. As much as the suggestion that Wright might have destroyed paperwork and then realized, when "outed," that he'd now have to reinstate it, stands, to a certain degree. But for many that's not enough. There have been just too many instances where discrepancies can't be explained to the extent that Wright's entire Satoshi claims must therefore be questioned.

"What do you say to the claims that many of your documents are fakes or forgeries?" I asked.

"I made a decision that we're not going to shut down anything that's truth, good, bad, or ugly. This is how things go wrong—when people don't address things and that makes me look bad. For instance, there's a lot of fake stuff from the ATO, so rather than avoiding it and saying it's not relevant you address it and say, one—they are not real documents, two—I had a series of audits."

"Are you saying your situation with the ATO isn't as it has been represented?" I asked.

"Well, my personal audit came back clean over a thirty-million-dollar turnover in my personal tax. It was right to the cent, despite the tax office having eight people digging through my fucking life in some kind of high-wealth individual witch-hunt. They found nothing and basically had to come back and apologize. They probably spent a million dollars trying to find something wrong with me."

"What about accusations of false R&D claims? How do you counter those?" I asked.

"They were done by KPMG who signed off at a partner level. I as CEO signed off on what the accountants told me. Then Ernst & Young did an external audit and signed off the other side. So we had two of the big accountants, plus another accountant, plus an internal audit. Everyone sits there saying 'Craig Wright did this' when actually my former boss at BDO, Allan Granger, ended up working with me with a whole number of staff working under him. But people don't listen to that. They just hear 'Craig Wright did a tax scam.'"

"So you were actually vindicated?"

"The issue at the time, now overturned, was that the ATO were arguing that GST should be paid on every Bitcoin transaction and I fought that. That caused me a lot of problems at the time. I told them they were wrong and it turned out that they were. It is now clear in law in Australia that there is no GST on Bitcoin. They just didn't like me personally or what I was doing. They also sued the Commonwealth Bank in Australia for the same thing. It took eight years and millions of dollars to go through the courts. Sometimes when a government decides they're going to fuck you over, you just bend over and get shafted."

"Do you have any regrets about anything?" I asked, as our Zoom credit ran down.

"If there's one thing, it's that I agreed to the deal with the devil that I took from Stefan and everyone, as much as I love him. Part of that deal was that I'd just be a scientist, working in the background. Well, I now know that doesn't work. My protocol, my vision; I'm the one who cares. I can't just sit there and leave everything to others. A lot of the problems we had were because people like Jimmy Nguyen wanted to be friendly with everyone. And you just can't be. This whole 'co-opetition' BS just doesn't work."

As I hung up my last Zoom call with Craig Wright, I must admit that I was left with an empty feeling.

Over several months of speaking with him and people in his world, it was pretty clear that he was the man who invented Bitcoin and who wrote the white paper. There is simply too much evidence to suggest that this was the case and almost no evidence to suggest that anybody else could have been more involved. To paraphrase what Andrew O'Hagan once said, Wright wasn't just in the right place at the right time; he was at the only place at the only time.

So, why the empty feeling? And why were there still doubts?

The answer there lies with Wright himself, I think. Craig Wright just does not make extracting information easy. Whether it's the way his mind works, his autism or his Asperger's, who knows. But there is something about how Wright explains events that makes what, on the surface, look plausible, implausible. Depending on the situation, he either adds too much detail or omits too much. It's hard to explain.

The net result is the same though: you're almost left with the perfect truth, but not quite—and maybe that's how a story like Bitcoin is meant to be, anyway. After all, for all the evidence at all the court cases and for all that it was compelling, not one piece of that evidence provided the "game over" moment that the Satoshi Nakamoto has promised to deliver for so long, but never has.

"I look at this way," Kurt Wuckert Jr. says, "Craig did his best to disappear himself and now that the game has shifted and he has to do his best to prove that he's Satoshi and it's probably basically impossible. But what do you do?"

Despite the doubts, the truth remains that Craig Wright most likely is, on all known evidence, Satoshi Nakamoto, the creator of Bitcoin. However, it is perhaps of no surprise whatsoever that a story like his should be shrouded in the kind of unknowns and dark hallways that it is given the internet age that we live in.

"I think Craig is fundamentally awkward about telling his story," Wuckert Jr. says. "And the reason for that is all the reasons why we should expect Satoshi to be less than honest about his story: the pseudonym was created to maintain a very important lie and that's what we should expect from this story. Craig knows that this was dark web, very, very dangerous stuff in many ways, and he pretends that it's not. I don't think he's being dishonest. But he's not telling you the very obvious risks that are associated with creating an internet money."

I couldn't help thinking about the backers, Calvin Ayre and Stefan Matthews, both of whom I had grown to like, in addition to still admiring their steadfast belief in Wright's story.

"As a businessperson, I know that to anyone smart just Craig's world-leading and growing patent portfolio make it impossible anyone other than him is Satoshi. This is why Craig has already won in history," says Ayre.

No matter what was happening out in the wider crypto world—whether an exchange like FTX went under spectacularly or whether BTC hit $68000—Ayre's and Matthew's position remained unchanged: that Craig Wright is Satoshi, BSV is the only Bitcoin, and everything else is an infringement of Wright's IP and liable to be enforced in court.

I was told that everything other than Satoshi's Bitcoin protocol was a scam and they meant it. The fall of crypto exchanges, with customers being burned for huge sums, would seem to confirm that Ayre's assessment back in May 2022 when we first met was nothing but accurate.

After all, if they didn't believe it all, there wouldn't be lawsuits in place accusing huge crypto-currency exchanges like Kraken and Coinbase of deceiving customers by "passing off" BTC and BCH as Bitcoin. Yet these things are already underway, and it clearly isn't just about the money.

"I can't see how it could be about the money for Craig's backers like Calvin and Stefan. It's been so stupidly expensive. In fact, to do this as a scam makes no sense for any of them," Wuckert Jr. says. "There is so much easy money to make in crypto. If the idea was just to trot out some cypherpunk and make easy money, it wouldn't look anything like this. There's so much money behind infrastructure and research; they clearly care about this. If they just wanted to make money, they could have brought out Craig Wright and said, 'Hey, here's this dude Craig Wright. He's a computer ninja.' Look what they did with Algorand. They've got Silvio Macali, everyone's very happy that he's there and saying, 'Buy our token and we're going to print a billion dollars out of nowhere,' and they did. If Calvin and Stefan wanted to do that with Craig they could have, and left Satoshi alone. There's no way this is about anything other than principle."

Whatever happens, Craig Wright's Bitcoin story will forever be central to the history of one of mankind's greatest ever technological inventions. And the men whose involvement saved it eight years ago deserve some recognition for the role they played.

Until someone else comes along to disprove it, Craig Wright's Satoshi Nakamoto narrative seems like the definitive one and there was no formal team at his side either. Dave Kleiman assisted,

Professor David Rees probably offered minimal advice and a few others might well have put an oar in along the way in some shape or form also. But really, all the evidence suggests that it all stops at Craig Wright.

"Dead people have families," Wright's tweet on February 15th, 2023, began. "The argument that there is someone else out there who could have created Bitcoin that is used to attack me is completely asinine," he continued. "If I wasn't Satoshi, Satoshi would discredit me."

ABOUT THE AUTHOR

Mark Eglinton is a Scottish author and cowriter. His recent books include *No Domain: The John McAfee Tapes*, which has optioned for cinematic release; *Blindsided* with former Australian rugby captain and stroke survivor Michael Lynagh, which was shortlisted for the Sports Book Award International Autobiography of the Year in 2016; *Heavy Duty: Days and Nights in Judas Priest* with musician K.K Downing, one of 2018's top ten music according to Rolling Stone; and *Reboot: My Life, My Time* with football legend Michael Owen, shortlisted for The Telegraph's Autobiography of the Year in 2020. Among other endeavors, Eglinton is a former professional golf caddie and has written about his experiences for *Golf* magazine and *Golf Digest*.